Best-Loved
WHOLE GRAIN
R E C I P E S

Publications International, Ltd.

Favorite Brand Name Recipes at www.fbnr.com

Microwave Cooking: Microwave ovens vary in wattage. Use the cooking times as guidelines and check for doneness before adding more time.

Preparation/Cooking Times: Preparation times are based on the approximate amount of time required to assemble the recipe before cooking, baking, chilling or serving. These times include preparation steps such as measuring, chopping and mixing. The fact that some preparations and cooking can be done simultaneously is taken into account. Preparation of optional ingredients and serving suggestions is not included.

contents

p. 5

p. 52

p. 238

hearty mornings

Start your day right by going with the grain. Homemade Fruited Granola or a hot, hearty bowl of Maple Apple Oatmeal can keep you energized long past lunchtime. Whole grains have more fiber, vitamins and minerals than refined grains, but the best reason to add them to your breakfast table is the taste. Whole grains have a nuttiness and hearty texture that make wimpy white bread or ordinary cereal seem boring in comparison.

fruited granola

3 cups uncooked quick oats
1 cup sliced almonds
1 cup honey
½ cup wheat germ or honey wheat germ
3 tablespoons butter or margarine, melted
1 teaspoon ground cinnamon
3 cups whole wheat cereal flakes
½ cup dried blueberries or golden raisins
½ cup dried cranberries or cherries
½ cup dried banana chips or chopped pitted dates

1. Preheat oven to 325°F.

2. Spread oats and almonds in single layer in 13×9-inch baking pan. Bake 15 minutes or until lightly toasted, stirring frequently.

3. Combine honey, wheat germ, butter and cinnamon in large bowl until well blended. Add oats and almonds; toss to coat completely. Spread mixture in single layer in baking pan. Bake 20 minutes or until golden brown. Cool completely in pan on wire rack. Break mixture into chunks.

4. Combine oat chunks, wheat cereal, blueberries, cranberries and banana chips in large bowl. Store in airtight container at room temperature up to 2 weeks. *Makes about 20 servings*

Tip: Prepare this granola on the weekend and you'll have a scrumptious snack or breakfast treat on hand for the rest of the week!

sunny seed bran waffles

     2 egg whites
     1 tablespoon packed dark brown sugar
     1 tablespoon vegetable oil
     1 cup fat-free (skim) milk
     ⅔ cup wheat bran
     ⅔ cup uncooked quick oats
     1½ teaspoons baking powder
     ¼ teaspoon salt
     3 tablespoons toasted sunflower seeds*
     1 cup apple butter

To toast sunflower seeds, cook and stir sunflower seeds in small nonstick skillet over medium heat about 5 minutes or until golden brown, stirring occasionally. Remove from skillet; let cool.

1. Beat egg whites in medium bowl with electric mixer until soft peaks form; set aside. Mix sugar and oil in small bowl. Stir in milk; mix well. Combine bran, oats, baking powder and salt in large bowl; mix well. Stir sugar mixture into bran mixture. Add sunflower seeds; stir just until moistened. *Do not overmix.* Gently fold in beaten egg whites.

2. Spray nonstick waffle iron lightly with nonstick cooking spray; heat according to manufacturer's directions. Stir batter; spoon ½ cup batter into waffle iron for each waffle. Cook until steam stops escaping from around edges and waffle is golden brown. Serve each waffle with ¼ cup apple butter.   *Makes 4 waffles*

Note: It is essential to use a nonstick waffle iron because of the low fat content of these waffles.

sunny seed bran waffle

breakfast bites

½ cup mascarpone cheese
2 tablespoons packed brown sugar
2 tablespoons heavy cream
¼ teaspoon almond extract
⅔ cup whole wheat pastry flour*
⅓ cup buckwheat flour
1 teaspoon baking powder
1 teaspoon granulated sugar
1 teaspoon ground cinnamon
¼ teaspoon salt
2 eggs
¼ to ⅓ cup water
1 teaspoon vanilla
   Fresh raspberries (optional)

Whole wheat pastry flour is available at natural food stores and some supermarkets.

1. For topping, combine mascarpone, brown sugar, cream and almond extract in small bowl; set aside.

2. Mix pastry flour, buckwheat flour, baking powder, granulated sugar, cinnamon and salt in medium bowl. Beat eggs, ¼ cup water and vanilla in another medium bowl until smooth. Whisk egg mixture into flour mixture, adding additional water 1 teaspoon at a time as needed to make thick batter.

3. Heat nonstick skillet or griddle. Drop about 2 tablespoons batter per pancake into skillet. Cook 2 to 3 minutes or until browned and puffy. Flip and cook another 2 to 3 minutes. Top each pancake with scant teaspoon of topping. Serve with fresh raspberries, if desired. *Makes 8 servings*

honey granola with yogurt

½ cup uncooked old-fashioned oats

¼ cup sliced almonds

2 tablespoons toasted wheat germ

1 tablespoon orange juice

1 tablespoon honey

½ teaspoon ground cinnamon

1½ cups whole strawberries

4 containers (6 ounces each) plain yogurt

1 teaspoon vanilla

1. Preheat oven to 325°F. Lightly spray 8-inch square baking pan with nonstick cooking spray; set aside.

2. Combine oats, almonds and wheat germ in small bowl. Combine orange juice, honey and cinnamon in another small bowl. Add juice mixture to oat mixture; mix well. Spread mixture evenly into prepared pan. Bake 20 to 25 minutes or until toasted, stirring twice during baking. Spread mixture on large sheet of foil to cool completely.

3. Cut 3 strawberries in half for garnish. Slice remaining strawberries. Combine yogurt and vanilla in medium bowl. Layer sliced strawberries, yogurt mixture and granola in 6 dessert dishes. Garnish with strawberry halves.   *Makes 6 servings*

Prep Time: 10 minutes
Bake Time: 20 to 25 minutes

honey granola with yogurt

harvest apple oatmeal

1 cup unsweetened apple juice
1 cup water
1 medium apple, cored and chopped
1 cup old-fashioned oats
¼ cup raisins
⅛ teaspoon salt
⅛ teaspoon ground cinnamon
    Apple slices (optional)

Microwave Directions

1. Combine juice, water and chopped apple in 2-quart microwavable bowl. Microwave on HIGH 3 minutes, stirring halfway through cooking time.

2. Add oats, raisins, salt and cinnamon; stir until well blended.

3. Microwave on MEDIUM 4 to 5 minutes or until thick; stir before serving. Garnish with apple slices. *Makes 2 servings*

Conventional Directions: Bring apple juice, water and chopped apple to a boil in medium saucepan over medium-high heat. Stir in oats, raisins, salt and cinnamon until well blended. Cook, uncovered, over medium heat 5 to 6 minutes or until thick, stirring occasionally.

harvest apple oatmeal

morning sandwich cookies

1 tablespoon butter or vegetable oil
¾ cup quick oats
¼ cup sliced almonds
1 cup whole wheat flour
1 cup peeled grated apple
1 cup shredded carrots
¼ cup pitted chopped prunes
⅓ cup egg substitute or egg whites
¼ cup milk
2 tablespoons sugar
½ teaspoon baking powder
¼ teaspoon baking soda
½ teaspoon ground cinnamon
¼ teaspoon ground nutmeg
6 teaspoons peanut butter
6 teaspoons raspberry fruit spread

1. Preheat oven to 425°F. Melt butter in small nonstick skillet over medium heat; add oats and almonds. Cook and stir 3 minutes; let cool.

2. Place oats, flour, apple, carrots, prunes, egg substitute, milk, sugar, baking powder, baking soda, cinnamon and nutmeg in food processor. Pulse until combined.

3. Spray 13×9-inch baking pan with nonstick cooking spray; press dough evenly into pan. Bake 20 minutes. Cool 15 minutes in pan on wire rack.

4. Cut into 12 pieces. Spread 6 pieces with peanut butter and raspberry spread. Top with remaining pieces to make sandwiches.   *Makes 6 cookies*

popcorn granola

1 cup quick oats

6 cups air-popped popcorn

1 cup golden raisins

½ cup (2 ounces) chopped mixed dried fruit

¼ cup (1 ounce) sunflower seeds

2 tablespoons butter

2 tablespoons packed light brown sugar

1 tablespoon honey

¼ teaspoon ground cinnamon

¼ teaspoon ground nutmeg

1. Preheat oven to 350°F. Spread oats on ungreased baking sheet; bake 10 to 15 minutes or until lightly toasted, stirring occasionally.

2. Combine oats, popcorn, raisins, dried fruit and sunflower seeds in large bowl. Heat butter, sugar, honey, cinnamon and nutmeg in small saucepan over medium heat until butter is melted. Drizzle over popcorn mixture; toss to coat.

Makes 8 servings

maple apple oatmeal

2 cups apple juice

1½ cups water

⅓ cup AUNT JEMIMA® Syrup

½ teaspoon ground cinnamon

¼ teaspoon salt (optional)

2 cups QUAKER® Oats (quick or old fashioned, uncooked)

1 cup chopped unpeeled apple (about 1 medium)

In a 3-quart saucepan, bring juice, water, syrup, cinnamon and, if desired, salt to a boil. Stir in oats and apple. Return to a boil; reduce heat to medium-low. Cook about 1 minute for quick oats (or 5 minutes for old fashioned oats) or until most of liquid is absorbed, stirring occasionally. Let stand until of desired consistency.

Makes 4 servings

popcorn granola

berry bran muffins

2 cups bran cereal

1¼ cups fat-free (skim) milk

½ cup packed brown sugar

¼ cup vegetable oil

1 egg, lightly beaten

1 teaspoon vanilla

1¼ cups all-purpose flour

1 tablespoon baking powder

¼ teaspoon salt

1 cup fresh or frozen blueberries (partially thawed if frozen)

1. Preheat oven to 350°F. Line 12 standard (2¾-inch) muffin cups with paper baking cups.

2. Mix cereal and milk in medium bowl. Let stand 5 minutes to soften. Add brown sugar, oil, egg and vanilla. Beat well. Combine flour, baking powder and salt in large bowl. Stir in cereal mixture just until dry ingredients are moistened. Gently fold in berries. Fill prepared muffin cups almost full.

3. Bake 20 to 25 minutes (25 to 30 if using frozen berries) or until toothpick inserted into centers comes out clean. Serve warm.   *Makes 12 muffins*

power breakfast

3 cups cooked brown rice

2 cups skim milk

¼ cup brown sugar

½ teaspoon cinnamon

½ cup whole milk

⅓ cup raisins

½ teaspoon vanilla extract

Sliced fresh fruit

¾ cup low-fat granola cereal (optional)

1 (6-ounce) container low-fat vanilla yogurt (optional)

Combine rice, skim milk, brown sugar and cinnamon in 2½- to 3-quart saucepan; heat over medium heat, stirring frequently, 10 to 12 minutes or until mixture thickens. Stir in whole milk, raisins and vanilla. Cook 5 minutes, stirring until mixture thickens slightly. Place rice mixture into serving bowls. Sprinkle with fruit. Top each serving with 2 tablespoons granola and yogurt, if desired.

Makes 6 servings

*Favorite recipe from **USA Rice***

banana coffee cake

½ cup 100% bran cereal

½ cup strong brewed coffee

1 cup mashed ripe bananas (about 2 bananas)

½ cup sugar

1 egg, lightly beaten

2 tablespoons canola or vegetable oil

½ cup all-purpose flour

½ cup whole wheat flour

2 teaspoons baking powder

1 teaspoon ground cinnamon

¼ teaspoon salt

1. Preheat oven to 350°F. Coat 8-inch square baking dish with nonstick cooking spray; set aside.

2. Combine bran cereal and coffee in large bowl; let stand 3 minutes or until cereal softens. Stir in bananas, sugar, egg and oil.

3. Combine all-purpose flour, whole wheat flour, baking powder, cinnamon and salt in small bowl; stir into banana mixture just until moistened. Pour into prepared pan.

4. Bake 25 to 35 minutes or until toothpick inserted into center of cake comes out clean. Cool in pan on wire rack. Cut into 9 squares before serving.

Makes 9 servings

country breakfast cereal

3 cups cooked brown rice
2 cups skim milk
½ cup raisins or chopped prunes
1 tablespoon margarine (optional)
1 teaspoon ground cinnamon
⅛ teaspoon salt
   Honey or brown sugar (optional)
   Fresh fruit (optional)

Combine rice, milk, raisins, margarine, cinnamon, and salt in 2- to 3-quart saucepan. Bring to a boil; stir once or twice. Reduce heat to medium-low; cover and simmer 8 to 10 minutes or until thickened. Serve with honey and fresh fruit.

Makes 6 servings

Favorite recipe from **USA Rice**

oat cakes with raspberry topping

1 pint raspberries
½ cup sugar, divided
2 tablespoons cornstarch
½ cup water
1 teaspoon lemon juice
½ cup quick oats
1 cup whole wheat flour
2½ teaspoons baking powder
1¼ cups fat-free (skim) milk
½ cup plain fat-free yogurt
   Nonstick cooking spray

1. Place half of raspberries in medium bowl; mash with potato masher. Set aside remaining raspberries.

2. Combine ⅓ cup sugar and cornstarch in small saucepan. Stir in water until smooth. Cook and stir over medium heat until mixture comes to a boil. Add lemon juice and mashed raspberries; return to a boil. Remove from heat; let stand 15 minutes. Stir in remaining raspberries.

3. Stir oats in heavy skillet over medium heat 3 minutes or until slightly browned. Place in medium bowl; cool 10 minutes. Stir in flour, baking powder and remaining sugar. Combine milk and yogurt in small bowl; stir into flour mixture just until all ingredients are moistened. (Batter will be lumpy.)

4. Coat nonstick griddle or heavy skillet with cooking spray. Heat over medium heat until water droplets sprinkled on griddle bounce off surface. Drop batter by scant ¼ cupfuls onto griddle; spread batter to form 4-inch round cakes. Cook 2 minutes or until top is covered with bubbles. Turn cakes; cook 2 minutes longer or until browned. Serve warm with raspberry topping. *Makes 6 servings*

Variation: Hulled, sliced strawberries or blueberries can be substituted for the raspberries.

oat cakes with raspberry topping

date-nut granola

2 cups old-fashioned oats
2 cups barley flakes
1 cup sliced almonds
⅓ cup vegetable oil
⅓ cup honey
1 teaspoon vanilla
1 cup chopped dates

1. Preheat oven to 350°F. Grease 13×9-inch baking pan.

2. Combine oats, barley flakes and almonds in large bowl; set aside.

3. Combine oil, honey and vanilla in small bowl. Pour honey mixture over oat mixture; stir well. Pour into prepared pan.

4. Bake about 25 minutes or until toasted, stirring frequently after the first 10 minutes. Stir in dates while mixture is still hot. Cool. Store tightly covered.

Makes 6 cups

Barley flakes, which are sometimes called rolled barley, are an excellent addition to your pantry. They look similar to old-fashioned oats (rolled oats) and are made in the same way, by steaming the grain and pressing through rollers. Like oats, barley flakes may be cooked for a tasty hot cereal. The dietary fiber in barley has been shown to help lower blood cholesterol.

date-nut granola

pea and spinach frittata

Nonstick cooking spray
1 cup chopped onion
¼ cup water
1 cup frozen peas
1 cup torn stemmed spinach
6 egg whites
2 eggs
½ cup cooked brown rice
¼ cup fat-free (skim) milk
2 tablespoons grated Romano or Parmesan cheese
1 tablespoon chopped fresh mint *or* 1 teaspoon dried mint
¼ teaspoon black pepper
⅛ teaspoon salt
Additional grated Romano or Parmesan cheese (optional)

1. Coat large skillet with nonstick cooking spray. Combine onion and water in skillet; bring to a boil over high heat. Reduce heat to medium. Cover; cook 2 to 3 minutes or until onion is tender. Stir in peas. Cook until peas are heated through; drain. Stir in spinach. Cook and stir about 1 minute or until spinach just starts to wilt.

2. Meanwhile, combine egg whites, eggs, rice, milk, 2 tablespoons Romano cheese, mint, pepper and salt in medium bowl. Add egg mixture to skillet. Cook, without stirring, 2 minutes until eggs begin to set. Run large spoon around edge of skillet, lifting eggs for even cooking. Remove skillet from heat when eggs are almost set but surface is still moist.

3. Cover; let stand 3 to 4 minutes or until surface is set. Sprinkle top with additional Romano cheese. Cut into 4 wedges to serve. *Makes 4 servings*

pea and spinach frittata

whole wheat popovers

1¼ cups whole wheat pastry flour*
1¼ cups milk
3 eggs
2 tablespoons melted butter
¼ teaspoon salt
1 tablespoon cold butter, cut into 6 pieces

*Whole wheat pastry flour is available at natural food stores and some supermarkets.

1. Position rack in lower third of oven. Preheat oven to 400°F. Spray popover pan with nonstick cooking spray. (If popover pan is not available, jumbo muffin pans or custard cups may be used.)

2. Place flour, milk, eggs, melted butter and salt in food processor or blender. Process until batter is smooth and consistency of heavy cream. (Batter may also be blended in large bowl with electric mixer.) Meanwhile, place popover pan in oven 2 minutes to preheat. Immediately place one piece of cold butter in each cup and return to oven 1 minute or until butter melts.

3. Fill each cup halfway with batter. Bake 20 minutes. *Do not open oven or popovers may fall. Reduce oven temperature to 300°F.* Bake 20 minutes more. Remove from pan; cool slightly on wire rack. Serve warm.   *Makes 6 popovers*

smoked ham corncakes with bean sauce

1 can (about 15 ounces) black beans, rinsed and drained
1 cup buttermilk, divided
2 tablespoons olive oil, divided
1 tablespoon balsamic vinegar
1 clove garlic, minced
1 teaspoon sugar
¼ teaspoon black pepper
¾ cup yellow cornmeal
¼ cup plus 2 tablespoons all-purpose flour
½ teaspoon baking soda
½ teaspoon salt
2 eggs, lightly beaten
6 tablespoons cream cheese, softened
1 cup corn, divided
⅔ cup chopped smoked ham
½ cup finely chopped fresh chives
   Sour cream and tomatoes (optional)

1. Combine beans, ¼ cup buttermilk, 1 tablespoon oil, vinegar, garlic, sugar and pepper in blender. Cover; blend until smooth.

2. Heat medium saucepan over low heat. Add bean mixture. Cook and stir 8 to 10 minutes until heated through; keep warm.

3. Meanwhile, combine cornmeal, flour, baking soda and salt in large bowl. Combine remaining ¾ cup buttermilk, eggs and cream cheese in blender. Cover; blend until smooth. Add ½ cup corn; blend until chopped. Stir buttermilk mixture, remaining corn, ham and chives into cornmeal mixture.

4. Heat remaining 1 tablespoon oil in large nonstick skillet over high heat. Drop ¼ cup batter into oil; spread to 4-inch circle with spoon. Cook 2 to 3 minutes on each side until golden brown. Repeat with remaining batter.

5. Serve corncakes with bean sauce, sour cream and tomatoes.

Makes 8 servings

smoked ham corncakes with bean sauce

buckwheat pancakes

2 cups buckwheat flour*
2 cups all-purpose flour
2 tablespoons sugar
4 teaspoons baking powder
2 teaspoons baking soda
1 teaspoon salt
1 cup milk
2 tablespoons butter, melted
1 egg, lightly beaten

*Buckwheat flour can be purchased in health food stores. Substitute whole wheat flour, if desired.

1. Combine buckwheat flour, all-purpose flour, sugar, baking powder, baking soda and salt in medium bowl; make well in center.

2. Whisk together milk, butter and egg in small bowl. Pour into flour mixture; stir just until blended. (Batter will have small lumps.)

3. Lightly grease griddle or skillet with additional butter or nonstick cooking spray. Heat griddle until hot.

4. Drop batter by ¼ cupfuls onto hot griddle. Cook 3 to 4 minutes or until bubbles appear and break on the surface of pancakes. Turn pancakes. Cook 3 to 4 minutes or until bottoms are browned. Serve immediately.   *Makes about 12 pancakes*

Buttermilk Pancakes: Substitute 1¼ cups buttermilk for milk.

Blueberry Pancakes: Fold ½ cup fresh or thawed, frozen blueberries into batter.

Buckwheat is not wheat. In fact, it's related to rhubarb, and is a flowering plant, not a cereal grass. The distinctively earthy taste of buckwheat shows up in whole toasted form as kasha. Buckwheat flour is used to make Japan's soba noodles. It is a good source of vitamins, minerals and protein.

Buckwheat
Pancakes

sturdy soups & salads

Whole grains can turn a simple soup or salad into a filling meal. Don't save these dishes for the side. Served with a loaf of crusty bread, Hoppin' John Soup or Mediterranean Barley Salad will satisfy even hearty appetites. Better yet, whole grains keep you satisfied longer because they're higher in fiber than refined grains. Nutrition may be the reason you add grains to your diet, but the bold flavors and textures will keep you coming back for more.

asian brown rice and peanut salad toss

1½ cups water
¾ cup uncooked brown rice
⅔ cup dry-roasted peanuts
1 can (8 ounces) sliced water chestnuts, drained
1 cup snow peas
½ cup chopped red onion
½ cup chopped green bell pepper
¼ cup dried cranberries or raisins
2 tablespoons cider vinegar
2 tablespoons honey
2 tablespoons reduced-sodium soy sauce
¼ teaspoon red pepper flakes

1. Bring water to a boil over high heat in medium saucepan. Stir in rice; return to a boil. Reduce heat; simmer, covered, 30 to 40 minutes or until rice is tender and liquid is absorbed. Rinse rice with cold water; drain well.

2. Meanwhile, place small skillet over medium-high heat. Add peanuts; cook and stir 3 to 4 minutes or until fragrant and beginning to brown. Transfer to large bowl. Stir in water chestnuts, snow peas, onion, bell pepper and cranberries. Stir in rice.

3. Combine vinegar, honey, soy sauce and pepper flakes in small bowl.

4. Add vinegar mixture to rice mixture; toss to coat.   *Makes 6 servings*

cremini mushroom and roasted garlic rice soup

½ cup butter
1 pound cremini mushrooms, sliced
1 large sweet mild onion, finely chopped
3 cups cooked brown rice, divided
1 (6½-ounce) container Garlic and Herbs Spreadable Cheese
2 (14-ounce) cans roasted garlic seasoned chicken broth, divided
2 cups water, additional if desired
8 slices pre-cooked ready-to-serve smoked bacon
    Salt and black pepper to taste

Melt butter in a large non-stick stockpot over medium-high heat. Add mushrooms and onion; cook about 10 minutes, stirring periodically. Let mixture cool slightly. In food processor or blender, combine mushroom mixture, 1½ cups rice, cheese and 1 cup broth. Pulse mixture until mushrooms are finely chopped but not pureed and mixture is thoroughly combined. Return mixture to stockpot; stir in remaining rice, broth and water. Bring to a boil; cook, uncovered, over medium heat 5 minutes. Heat bacon slices between paper towels in microwave according to package directions. Chop bacon and set aside. Add salt and pepper to soup to taste. To serve, ladle soup into bowls; sprinkle with bacon. *Makes 8 to 12 servings*

Favorite recipe from **USA Rice**

 *grain of advice*

Cooked brown rice can be refrigerated for several days or frozen for up to 3 months, so it pays to make enough for leftovers. To reheat frozen rice, microwave on HIGH in a covered microwavable dish for 1 to 2 minutes, stirring once, or thaw overnight in the refrigerator.

cremini mushroom and
roasted garlic rice soup

mediterranean barley salad

1⅓ cups water
⅔ cup quick-cooking barley
½ cup diced roasted red peppers
12 pitted kalamata olives, coarsely chopped
12 turkey pepperoni slices, halved
¼ cup chopped red onion
2 ounces crumbled feta cheese
1 teaspoon dried basil
¼ teaspoon dried red pepper flakes
1 can (about 15 ounces) navy beans
1 can (14 ounces) sliced hearts of palm, drained
1 tablespoon extra-virgin olive oil
1 tablespoon cider vinegar
Salt and black pepper

1. Bring water to a boil in medium saucepan over high heat. Add barley; return to a boil. Reduce heat, cover tightly and simmer 10 minutes or until barley is tender.

2. Meanwhile, combine roasted peppers, olives, pepperoni, onion, feta, basil and red pepper flakes in medium bowl.

3. Place barley and beans in colander; run under cold water until barley is cool and beans are rinsed. Add barley, beans and hearts of palm to roasted pepper mixture.

4. Stir in oil and vinegar. Season with salt and pepper; refrigerate until serving.

Makes 4 servings

salmon, corn and barley chowder

1 teaspoon canola oil
¼ cup chopped onion
1 clove garlic, minced
2½ cups reduced-sodium chicken broth
¼ cup quick-cooking barley
1 tablespoon water
1 tablespoon all-purpose flour
1 can (4 ounces) salmon, drained
1 cup frozen corn, thawed
⅓ cup reduced-fat (2%) milk
½ teaspoon chili powder
¼ teaspoon ground cumin
¼ teaspoon dried oregano
⅛ teaspoon salt
1 tablespoon minced fresh cilantro
⅛ teaspoon black pepper
   Lime wedges (optional)

1. Heat oil in medium saucepan over medium heat. Add onion and garlic. Cook and stir 1 to 2 minutes or until onion is tender.

2. Add broth; bring to a boil. Stir in barley. Cover; reduce heat and simmer 10 minutes or until barley is tender.

3. Stir water gradually into flour in small bowl until smooth; set aside. Remove and discard bones and skin from salmon; flake into bite-size pieces.

4. Add salmon, corn and milk to saucepan; stir until blended. Stir in flour paste, chili powder, cumin, oregano and salt. Simmer gently 2 to 3 minutes or until slightly thickened. Stir in cilantro and pepper. Serve with lime wedges, if desired.

Makes 2 (2¼-cup) servings

salmon, corn and barley chowder

hoppin' john soup

1 bag SUCCESS® Brown Rice
¼ pound spicy turkey sausage
½ cup chopped onion
½ pound turnips, peeled and chopped
2 carrots, peeled and chopped
½ teaspoon salt
½ teaspoon black pepper
3 cups chicken broth
1 package (8 ounces) frozen black-eyed peas, thawed and drained
1 package (8 ounces) frozen chopped mustard greens, thawed and drained
½ teaspoon red pepper flakes

Prepare rice according to package directions. Brown sausage in large saucepan or Dutch oven over medium-high heat; drain. Add onion, turnips, carrots, salt and pepper. Reduce heat to low; simmer 7 minutes. Add broth; simmer 5 minutes. Add rice, peas and greens; simmer 10 minutes, stirring occasionally. Sprinkle with red pepper flakes.   *Makes 6 servings*

country stew

2 bags SUCCESS® Brown Rice
1 pound ground turkey
1 small onion, chopped
2 cans (14½ ounces each) tomatoes, cut up, undrained
1 teaspoon pepper
½ teaspoon dried basil leaves, crushed
½ teaspoon garlic powder
1 can (16 ounces) whole kernel corn, drained

Prepare rice according to package directions. Brown ground turkey with onion in large skillet, stirring to separate turkey. Add tomatoes, pepper, basil and garlic powder; simmer 20 minutes, stirring occasionally. Stir in rice and corn; heat thoroughly, stirring occasionally.   *Makes 8 servings*

hoppin' john soup

wheat berry apple salad

  1 cup uncooked wheat berries (whole wheat kernels)
½ teaspoon salt
  2 apples (1 red and 1 golden)
½ cup dried cranberries
⅓ cup chopped walnuts
  1 stalk celery, chopped
    Grated peel and juice of 1 medium orange
  2 tablespoons rice wine vinegar
1½ tablespoons chopped fresh mint (1 bunch)
    Lettuce leaves (optional)

1. Place wheat berries and salt in large saucepan and cover by 1 inch with water.* Bring to a boil; stir. Reduce heat to low. Cover; cook stirring occasionally, for 1 hour or until wheat berries are tender but chewy. (Add additional water if wheat berries become dry during cooking.) Drain and let cool. (Refrigerate for up to 4 days if not using immediately.)

2. Cut unpeeled apples into bite-size pieces. Place wheat berries in large bowl; add apples, cranberries, walnuts, celery, orange peel, orange juice, vinegar and mint. Stir to combine. Cover; refrigerate at least 1 hour to allow flavors to blend. Serve on lettuce leaves.   *Makes about 6 cups*

*To cut cooking time by 20 to 30 minutes, wheat berries may be soaked in water overnight. Drain and cover with fresh water by 1 inch before cooking as above.

Wheat berries are simply uncooked whole kernels of wheat that have not been processed. They can be purchased from the bulk bins of large supermarkets and health food stores or by mail-order. Cooked wheat berries have a mild, nutty flavor and hearty texture that works well in a main course salad. Spelt or kamut, two other forms of whole wheat, may be substituted.

wheat berry apple salad

greens, white bean and barley soup

2 tablespoons olive oil

3 to 4 carrots, diced

1½ cups chopped onions

2 cloves garlic, minced

1½ cups sliced mushrooms

6 cups vegetable broth

2 cups cooked pearl barley

1 can (about 15 ounces) Great Northern beans, rinsed and drained

2 bay leaves

1 teaspoon sugar

1 teaspoon dried thyme

7 cups stemmed chopped collard greens

1 tablespoon white wine vinegar

Hot pepper sauce

Red bell pepper strips (optional)

1. Heat oil in Dutch oven over medium heat. Add carrots, onions and garlic; cook and stir 3 minutes. Add mushrooms; cook and stir 5 minutes or until carrots are tender.

2. Add broth, barley, beans, bay leaves, sugar and thyme. Bring to a boil over high heat. Reduce heat; simmer, covered, 5 minutes. Add greens; simmer 10 minutes. Remove and discard bay leaves. Stir in vinegar. Season to taste with pepper sauce. Garnish with red bell peppers strips. *Makes 8 (1¼-cup) servings*

greens, white bean and barley soup

tabbouleh in tomato cups

4 large firm ripe tomatoes (about 8 ounces each)
2 tablespoons olive oil
4 green onions, thinly sliced
1 cup uncooked bulgur wheat
1 cup water
2 tablespoons lemon juice
1 tablespoon chopped fresh mint leaves *or* ½ teaspoon dried mint
  Salt and pepper

1. Cut tomatoes in half crosswise. Scoop pulp and seeds out of tomatoes into medium bowl, leaving ¼-inch-thick shells.

2. Invert tomatoes on paper towel lined plate; drain 20 minutes. Meanwhile, chop tomato pulp; set aside.

3. Heat oil in medium saucepan over medium-high heat. Cook and stir green onions 1 to 2 minutes until wilted. Add bulgur; cook 3 to 5 minutes until browned.

4. Add reserved tomato pulp, water, lemon juice and mint to bulgur mixture. Bring to a boil over high heat; reduce heat to medium-low. Cover; simmer gently 15 to 20 minutes until liquid is absorbed. Season with salt and pepper. Fill tomato halves with mixture.*

5. Preheat oven to 400°F. Place filled cups in 13×9-inch baking dish; bake 15 minutes or until heated through.   *Makes 4 main-dish or 8 side-dish servings*

*Tomato cups may be covered and refrigerated up to 24 hours at this point.

italian beef and barley soup

1 boneless beef top sirloin steak (about 1½ pounds)
1 tablespoon vegetable oil
4 medium carrots or parsnips, cut into ¼-inch slices
1 cup chopped onion
1 teaspoon dried thyme
½ teaspoon dried rosemary
¼ teaspoon black pepper
⅓ cup uncooked pearl barley
2 cans (14½ ounces each) beef broth
1 can (14½ ounces) diced tomatoes with Italian seasoning

Slow Cooker Directions

1. Cut beef into 1-inch pieces. Heat oil in large skillet over medium-high heat. Brown beef on all sides; set aside.

2. Place carrots and onion in slow cooker; sprinkle with thyme, rosemary and pepper. Top with barley and meat. Pour broth and tomatoes over meat.

3. Cover; cook on LOW 8 to 10 hours or until beef is tender.   *Makes 6 servings*

Tip: Choose pearl barley rather than quick-cooking barley because it will stand up to long cooking.

Prep Time: 20 minutes
Cook Time: 8 to 10 hours

quinoa and mango salad

2 cups water

1 cup uncooked quinoa*

2 cups cubed peeled mangoes (about 2 large mangoes)

½ cup sliced green onions

½ cup dried cranberries

2 tablespoons chopped parsley

¼ cup olive oil

1 tablespoon plus 1½ teaspoons white wine vinegar

1 teaspoon Dijon mustard

½ teaspoon salt

⅛ teaspoon black pepper

Pronounced keen-wa. It is available in health food stores or in the health food aisle of large supermarkets.

1. Combine water and quinoa in medium saucepan. Bring to a boil. Reduce heat; simmer, covered, 10 to 12 minutes until all water is absorbed. Stir; let stand, covered, 15 minutes. Transfer to large bowl; cover and refrigerate at least 1 hour.

2. Add mango, green onions, cranberries and parsley to quinoa; mix well.

3. Combine oil, vinegar, mustard, salt and pepper in small bowl; whisk until blended. Pour over quinoa mixture; mix until well blended.   *Makes 8 (⅔-cup) servings*

Tip: This salad can be made several hours ahead and refrigerated. Allow it to stand at room temperature for at least 30 minutes before serving.

grain of advice

While quinoa is an ancient grain that was grown by the Incas, it is new to most Americans. This tiny round whole grain is higher in protein than other grains. It contains all eight essential amino acids; therefore, it is considered a complete protein.

quinoa and mango salad

mushroom barley stew

1 tablespoon olive oil
1 medium onion, finely chopped
1 cup chopped carrots (about 2 carrots)
1 clove garlic, minced
1 cup uncooked pearl barley
1 cup dried mushrooms, broken into pieces
1 teaspoon salt
½ teaspoon black pepper
½ teaspoon dried thyme
5 cups reduced-sodium vegetable broth

Slow Cooker Directions

1. Heat oil in medium skillet over medium-high heat. Add onion, carrots and garlic; cook and stir 5 minutes or until tender. Place in slow cooker.

2. Add barley, mushrooms, salt, pepper and thyme to slow cooker. Stir in broth.

3. Cover; cook on LOW 6 to 7 hours. Adjust seasonings before serving.

Makes 4 to 6 servings

Variation: To turn this thick robust stew into a soup, add 2 to 3 additional cups of broth. Cook the same length of time.

Prep Time: 10 minutes
Cook Time: 6 to 7 hours

wild rice and mixed greens salad

4 cups mixed baby greens
3 ounces baked or poached salmon or chicken
⅓ cup cooked brown and wild rice mixture*
2 tablespoons prepared reduced-fat salad dressing

Cook rice in reduced-sodium chicken broth for extra flavor.

Arrange greens on serving plate. Top with salmon. Sprinkle rice mixture over salmon and greens. Drizzle with dressing.   *Makes 1 serving*

santa fe salad

2 cups cooked brown rice, cooled
1 can (16 ounces) black beans or pinto beans, rinsed and drained
1 can (17 ounces) whole kernel corn, drained
¼ cup minced onion
¼ cup white vinegar
2 tablespoons vegetable oil
2 tablespoons snipped cilantro
2 jalapeño peppers, minced
2 teaspoons chili powder
1 teaspoon salt

Combine rice, beans, corn, and onion in medium bowl. Combine vinegar, oil, cilantro, peppers, chili powder, and salt in small jar with lid. Pour over rice mixture; toss lightly. Cover and chill 2 to 3 hours so flavors will blend. Stir before serving.

Makes 4 servings

*Favorite recipe from **USA Rice***

wild rice and mixed greens salad

simple turkey soup

2 pounds ground turkey, cooked and drained
1 can (about 28 ounces) whole tomatoes, undrained
2 cans (about 14 ounces each) beef broth
1 bag (16 ounces) frozen mixed soup vegetables, thawed
½ cup uncooked pearl barley
1 teaspoon salt
1 teaspoon dried thyme
½ teaspoon ground coriander
   Black pepper

Slow Cooker Directions

Combine all ingredients in 5-quart slow cooker. Add water to cover. Cover; cook on HIGH 3 to 4 hours. *Makes 8 servings*

Variation: Try adding other frozen or canned vegetables or extra diced potatoes and carrots. Sliced, diced or stewed tomatoes can be substituted for the whole tomatoes.

healthy brown rice salad

1 bag SUCCESS® Brown Rice
1 can (16 ounces) black-eyed peas, rinsed and drained
1 cup chopped celery
1 medium green bell pepper, chopped
1 medium red bell pepper, chopped
1 small red onion, chopped
1 clove garlic, minced
¼ cup low-fat Italian dressing

Prepare rice according to package directions. Cool.

Place rice in large bowl. Add remaining ingredients; mix lightly. Refrigerate 1 hour.
Makes 4 servings

spicy vegetable chili

½ cup uncooked wheat berries
    Nonstick cooking spray
 1 large onion, chopped
½ green bell pepper, chopped
½ yellow or red bell pepper, chopped
 2 stalks celery, sliced
 3 cloves garlic, minced
 1 can (14½ ounces) chopped tomatoes
 1 can (about 15 ounces) red kidney beans, rinsed and drained
 1 can (about 15 ounces) chickpeas, rinsed and drained
¾ cup raisins
½ cup water
 1 tablespoon chili powder
 1 teaspoon dried oregano
 1 tablespoon chopped fresh parsley
1½ teaspoons hot pepper sauce

1. Place wheat berries in small saucepan and cover with 2 cups water; let soak overnight. Bring to a boil over high heat. Reduce heat to low; cover and simmer 45 minutes to 1 hour or until wheat berries are tender. Drain; set aside.

2. Spray large saucepan or Dutch oven with cooking spray; heat over medium heat. Add onion; cover and cook 5 minutes. Add bell peppers, celery and garlic; cover and cook 5 minutes, stirring occasionally.

3. Add tomatoes, kidney beans, chickpeas, raisins, ½ cup water, chili seasoning, oregano and wheat berries to saucepan; mix well. Bring to a boil over high heat. Reduce heat to low; simmer 25 to 30 minutes, stirring occasionally. Stir in parsley and hot pepper sauce just before serving.   *Makes 4 servings*

bean salad with bulgur

¾ cup uncooked dried red kidney beans, sorted and rinsed

¾ cup uncooked dried pinto beans, sorted and rinsed

 8 ounces fresh green beans, cut into 2-inch pieces (about 1½ cups)

½ cup uncooked bulgur wheat

 1 cup water

⅓ cup vegetable oil

 1 tablespoon dark sesame oil

 6 green onions with tops, chopped

 2 tablespoons minced fresh ginger

 3 cloves garlic, minced

¼ teaspoon red pepper flakes

 3 tablespoons soy sauce

 2 tablespoons white wine vinegar

½ teaspoon sugar

1. Soak kidney and pinto beans overnight in cold water; rinse and drain. Place in large saucepan and cover with 6 cups water. Bring to a boil. Reduce heat to low; simmer, covered, 1 hour or until tender. Rinse and drain; set aside.

2. Meanwhile, place green beans in medium saucepan; cover with water. Bring to a boil over medium-high heat. Reduce heat to low; simmer, covered, 5 to 6 minutes until beans are crisp-tender. Rinse and drain; set aside.

3. Combine bulgur and 1 cup water in small saucepan. Bring to a boil over medium heat. Reduce heat to low; simmer, covered, 5 to 10 minutes or until water is absorbed and bulgur is fluffy.

4. Combine green beans, bulgur, kidney and pinto beans in large bowl.

5. Heat vegetable oil and sesame oil in large skillet over medium heat. Add onions, ginger, garlic and red pepper flakes. Cook and stir about 3 minutes or until onions are tender. Remove from heat. Stir in soy sauce, vinegar and sugar. Pour oil mixture into bean mixture; mix well. Cover; refrigerate 2 to 3 hours.

Makes 6 to 8 servings

muffins
& more

Quick breads and muffins are some of the most delicious uses for whole grains. The nutty flavor of whole wheat is the perfect addition to a rich banana bread or delectable pumpkin muffin. The flavor of the wheat complements fruits or spices instead of disappearing into the background like ho-hum white flour. Try Rosemary Breadsticks or Spiced Orange Cranberry Muffins and convert the family to whole grain goodness.

ripe banana muffins

2 cups whole wheat flour
¾ cup wheat bran (not bran cereal flakes)
¾ cup sugar
½ cup wheat germ
2 teaspoons ground cinnamon
1½ teaspoons baking soda
1 teaspoon baking powder
½ teaspoon salt
1½ to 1⅔ cups very ripe mashed bananas (3 or 4 bananas)
1 cup plain yogurt
1 egg, beaten
3 tablespoons vegetable oil
1 teaspoon vanilla
¾ cup chopped walnuts
¾ cup chocolate chips
⅓ cup raisins

1. Preheat oven to 350°F. Spray 12 standard (2¾-inch) muffin cups with nonstick cooking spray or line with paper baking cups.

2. Combine flour, bran, sugar, wheat germ, cinnamon, baking soda, baking powder and salt in medium bowl. Place bananas, yogurt, egg, oil and vanilla in large bowl; stir to blend thoroughly.

3. Add dry ingredients to banana mixture; stir just until combined. Stir in walnuts, chocolate chips and raisins. Spoon evenly into prepared muffin cups.

4. Bake 18 to 20 minutes or until toothpick inserted into centers comes out clean. Cool in pan 5 minutes on wire rack; remove to rack to cool.

Makes 12 muffins

soda bread

1½ cups whole wheat flour
1 cup all-purpose flour
½ cup rolled oats
¼ cup sugar
1½ teaspoons baking powder
½ teaspoon baking soda
¼ teaspoon ground cinnamon
⅓ cup raisins (optional)
¼ cup walnuts (optional)
1¼ cups low-fat buttermilk
1 tablespoon vegetable oil

Preheat oven to 375°F. Combine whole wheat flour, all-purpose flour, oats, sugar, baking powder, baking soda and cinnamon in large bowl. Stir in raisins and walnuts, if desired. Gradually stir in buttermilk and oil until dough forms. Knead in bowl for 30 seconds. Spray 8×4-inch loaf pan with nonstick cooking spray; place dough in pan. Bake 40 to 50 minutes or until wooden toothpick inserted into center comes out clean. *Makes 16 slices*

Favorite recipe from **The Sugar Association, Inc.**

spiced orange cranberry muffins

½ cup chopped cranberries

3 tablespoons packed brown sugar

1 cup orange juice

1 egg white

2 tablespoons vegetable oil

1 cup whole wheat flour

½ cup all-purpose flour

1½ teaspoons baking powder

½ teaspoon ground cinnamon

¼ teaspoon ground nutmeg

1. Preheat oven to 400°F. Grease 8 standard (2¾-inch) muffin cups or line with paper baking cups. Combine cranberries and sugar in small bowl; let stand 5 minutes. Stir in orange juice, egg white and oil.

2. Combine whole wheat flour, all-purpose flour, baking powder, cinnamon and nutmeg in medium bowl. Add cranberry mixture to flour mixture; stir just until combined. Spoon batter into prepared muffin cups, filling three-fourths full.

3. Bake 18 to 20 minutes or until toothpick inserted into centers comes out clean. Immediately remove from pan; cool on wire rack. *Makes 8 muffins*

spiced orange cranberry muffins

honey muffins

1 can (8 ounces) DOLE® Crushed Pineapple
1½ cups wheat bran cereal (not flakes)
⅔ cup buttermilk
1 egg, lightly beaten
⅓ cup chopped pecans or walnuts
3 tablespoons vegetable oil
½ cup honey, divided
⅔ cup whole wheat flour
½ teaspoon baking soda
⅛ teaspoon salt

Microwave Directions

Combine undrained crushed pineapple, cereal and buttermilk in large bowl. Let stand 10 minutes until cereal has absorbed liquid. Stir in egg, pecans, oil and ¼ cup honey. Combine flour, baking soda and salt in small bowl. Stir into bran mixture until just moistened. Spoon one half batter into 6 prepared cups,* filling to the top.

Microwave at HIGH (100%) for 3½ to 4 minutes, rotating pan ½ turn after 1½ minutes. Muffins are done when they look dry and set on top. Remove from oven; immediately spoon 1 teaspoon of remaining honey over each muffin. Remove to cooling rack after honey has been absorbed. Repeat procedure with remaining batter and honey. Serve warm.   *Makes 12 muffins*

Line six microwavable muffin cups or six 6-ounce microwavable custard cups with double thickness paper baking cups. (Outer cup will absorb moisture so inner cup sticks to cooked muffin.)

chive whole wheat drop biscuits

1¼ cups whole wheat flour
¾ cup all-purpose flour
3 tablespoons toasted wheat germ, divided
1 tablespoon baking powder
1 tablespoon chopped fresh chives *or* 1 teaspoon dried chives
2 teaspoons sugar
3 tablespoons cold butter
1 cup milk
½ cup shredded American or Cheddar cheese

1. Preheat oven to 450°F. Spray baking sheet with nonstick cooking spray; set aside.

2. Combine whole wheat flour, all-purpose flour, 2 tablespoons wheat germ, baking powder, chives and sugar in medium bowl. Cut in butter with pastry blender or two knives until mixture resembles coarse meal. Add milk and cheese; stir until just combined.

3. Drop dough by rounded teaspoonfuls about 1 inch apart onto prepared baking sheet. Sprinkle with remaining 1 tablespoon wheat germ. Bake 10 to 12 minutes or until golden brown. Remove immediately from baking sheet. Serve warm.

Makes 12 servings

Wheat germ is the heart of the wheat kernel and a concentrated source of nutrients. It is also part of the wheat that is eliminated when making processed white flour. Because they contain the oil-rich germ, whole wheat flour and wheat germ are both more perishable than processed white flour, so store them, well-wrapped, in your refrigerator or freezer to keep them fresh.

chive whole wheat drop biscuits

miniature fruit muffins

  1 cup whole wheat flour
¾ cup all-purpose flour
½ cup packed dark brown sugar
  2 teaspoons baking powder
½ teaspoon baking soda
¼ teaspoon salt
  1 cup buttermilk, divided
¾ cup frozen blueberries
  1 small ripe banana, mashed
¼ teaspoon vanilla
⅓ cup unsweetened applesauce
  2 tablespoons raisins
½ teaspoon ground cinnamon

1. Preheat oven to 400°F. Spray 36 mini (1¾-inch) muffin cups with nonstick cooking spray.

2. Combine flours, sugar, baking powder, baking soda and salt in medium bowl. Place ⅔ cup dry ingredients in each of 3 small bowls.

3. To first bowl of flour mixture, add ⅓ cup buttermilk and blueberries. Stir just until blended; spoon into 12 prepared muffin cups. To second bowl, add ⅓ cup buttermilk, banana and vanilla. Stir just until blended; spoon into 12 more prepared muffin cups. To third bowl, add remaining ⅓ cup buttermilk, applesauce, raisins and cinnamon. Stir just until blended; spoon into remaining 12 prepared muffin cups.

4. Bake 18 minutes or until lightly browned and toothpick inserted into centers comes out clean. Remove from pan. Cool 10 minutes on wire racks.

Makes 36 mini muffins

miniature fruit muffins

golden apricot muffins

1 cup all-purpose flour, divided
1 cup whole wheat flour
¼ cup sugar
1 teaspoon baking powder
1 teaspoon baking soda
¼ teaspoon salt
1 cup plain fat-free yogurt
½ cup puréed apricots
2 tablespoons vegetable oil
1 cup diced apricots

1. Preheat oven to 400°F. Line 12 standard (2¾-inch) muffin cups with paper baking cups or spray with nonstick cooking spray.

2. Reserve 1 tablespoon all-purpose flour. Combine remaining all-purpose flour, whole wheat flour, sugar, baking powder, baking soda and salt in medium bowl; mix well. Combine yogurt, puréed apricots and oil in small bowl; mix well. Add yogurt mixture to dry ingredients; stir just until moistened.

3. Toss diced apricots with reserved flour. Gently stir diced apricot mixture into batter. *Do not overmix.* Spoon batter into muffin cups, filling three-fourths full.

4. Bake 20 to 25 minutes or until toothpick inserted into centers of muffins comes out clean. Immediately remove from pan; cool on wire rack.   *Makes 12 muffins*

mott's® cinnamania bread

½ cup GRANDMA'S® Molasses

½ cup water

1 cup chopped dates

1 (4-ounce) container red cinnamon imperial candies

½ cup MOTT'S® Natural Apple Sauce

2 egg whites

1 teaspoon baking soda

1 teaspoon baking powder

3 teaspoons cinnamon

½ cup unprocessed bran

1½ cups whole wheat flour

Topping

¼ cup MOTT'S® Natural Apple Sauce

½ teaspoon cinnamon

¼ cup crushed walnuts

1. Preheat oven to 350°F. Spray 8½×4½×2½-inch loaf pan with nonstick cooking spray.

2. Combine Grandma's Molasses, water, dates and candies in microwavable bowl. Microwave for 4 minutes on high power or until boiling. Stir in ½ cup Mott's Natural Apple Sauce and let mixture cool approximately 15 minutes. Stir in egg whites.

3. In separate large bowl, mix together baking soda, baking powder, 3 teaspoons cinnamon, bran and wheat flour. Pour in molasses mixture and stir just until moistened.

4. Pour batter into prepared loaf pan. Prepare Topping. Mix together ¼ cup Mott's Natural Apple Sauce and ½ teaspoon cinnamon. Spread evenly over top of batter with the back of spoon. Sprinkle crushed walnuts on top. Bake for 1 hour or until knife inserted in center comes out clean. *Makes 9 servings*

sesame crunch banana muffins

   Sesame Crunch Topping (recipe follows)
2 ripe medium bananas, mashed
1 cup low-fat milk
2 egg whites
2 tablespoons vegetable oil
1 teaspoon vanilla extract
1½ cups uncooked rolled oats
½ cup all-purpose flour
½ cup whole wheat flour
2 tablespoons granulated sugar
1 tablespoon baking powder
½ teaspoon salt

1. Prepare Sesame Crunch Topping; set aside. Spray muffin cups with nonstick cooking spray or use paper liners. Preheat oven to 400°F.

2. Combine bananas, milk, egg whites, oil and vanilla in large bowl. Combine oats, flours, sugar, baking powder and salt in medium bowl; stir into banana mixture until just moistened. Fill prepared muffin cups about ¾ full. Sprinkle Topping evenly over batter in each cup. Bake 20 to 25 minutes until golden on top and wooden toothpick inserted into centers comes out clean. Cool slightly in pan before transferring to wire rack. *Makes about 16 muffins*

sesame crunch topping

4 tablespoons packed brown sugar
2 tablespoons chopped walnuts
2 tablespoons whole wheat flour
1 tablespoon sesame seeds
1 tablespoon margarine
¾ teaspoon ground nutmeg
¾ teaspoon ground cinnamon

Combine all ingredients; mix well.

Favorite recipes from **The Sugar Association, Inc.**

sesame crunch banana muffins

rosemary breadsticks

⅔ cup reduced-fat (2%) milk

¼ cup finely snipped fresh chives

2 teaspoons baking powder

1 teaspoon finely chopped fresh rosemary *or* ½ teaspoon dried rosemary

¾ teaspoon salt

½ teaspoon freshly ground black pepper

¾ cup whole wheat flour

¾ cup all-purpose flour

Nonstick cooking spray

1. Combine milk, chives, baking powder, rosemary, salt and pepper in large bowl; mix well. Stir in flours, ½ cup at a time, until blended. Turn onto floured surface and knead dough about 5 minutes or until smooth and elastic, adding more flour if dough is sticky. Let stand 30 minutes at room temperature.

2. Preheat oven to 375°F. Spray baking sheet with cooking spray. Divide dough into 12 equal pieces. Roll each piece into long thin rope; place on prepared baking sheet. Lightly spray breadsticks with cooking spray. Bake about 12 minutes or until bottoms are golden brown. Turn breadsticks over; bake about 10 minutes more or until golden brown. *Makes 12 breadsticks*

colusa corn muffins

¾ cup plain yogurt
⅓ cup butter or margarine, melted
½ cup honey
2 eggs
¾ cup all-purpose flour
¾ cup whole wheat flour
¾ cup cornmeal
2½ teaspoons baking powder
½ teaspoon salt
½ teaspoon baking soda

Beat together yogurt, butter, honey and eggs in small bowl. Set aside. Combine flours, cornmeal, baking powder, salt and baking soda in large bowl. Add honey mixture. Stir just enough to barely moisten flour. *Do not overmix.* Spoon batter into paper-lined or greased muffin cups.

Bake in preheated 350°F oven 20 to 25 minutes or until wooden toothpick inserted near center comes out clean. Remove from pan; cool slightly on wire racks. Serve warm. *Makes 1 dozen muffins*

Favorite recipe from **National Honey Board**

grain of advice

Cornmeal is produced by grinding dried corn kernels. If it is stone-ground, more of the germ and the hull of the corn are retained. This whole grain cornmeal is more nutritious, but also more perishable and should be stored in the refrigerator or freezer. Cornmeal that is labeled "degerminated" has been processed to remove the germ or heart of the kernel along with its nutrients.

colusa corn muffins

whole wheat pumpkin muffins

1⅓ cups all-purpose flour
¾ cup whole wheat flour
3 tablespoons sugar substitute*
1½ teaspoons baking powder
1 teaspoon pumpkin pie spice
½ teaspoon baking soda
½ teaspoon salt
1 cup solid-pack pumpkin
⅔ cup orange juice
2 eggs, beaten
¼ cup canola oil
3 tablespoons honey

This recipe was tested with sucralose-based sugar substitute.

1. Preheat oven to 400°F. Spray 12 standard (2¾-inch) muffin cups with nonstick cooking spray.

2. Combine all-purpose flour, whole wheat flour, sugar substitute, baking powder, pumpkin pie spice, baking soda and salt in large bowl. Combine pumpkin, orange juice, eggs, oil and honey in medium bowl. Add to dry ingredients, stirring just until moistened. Spoon batter evenly into prepared muffin cups.

3. Bake 15 to 20 minutes or until toothpick inserted into centers comes out clean. Cool in pan on wire rack 5 minutes. Remove from pan. Serve warm.

Makes 12 muffins

Prep Time: 15 minutes
Bake Time: 15 minutes

whole wheat tortillas

1½ cups whole wheat flour

½ cup all-purpose flour

1 teaspoon baking powder

½ teaspoon salt

¼ cup shortening

½ cup warm water

1. Combine flours, baking powder and salt in medium bowl. With fingers, pastry blender or 2 knives, rub or cut in shortening until mixture resembles fine crumbs. Gradually add water; stir with fork until mixture forms dough. Turn out onto lightly floured board; knead 2 minutes or until smooth. Shape into a ball; cover with bowl and let rest 30 minutes.

2. Divide dough into 8 equal portions for 9-inch tortillas or 12 portions for 6-inch tortillas. Keep dough covered to prevent it from drying out. Roll out one portion at a time on lightly floured board into ⅛-inch-thick circle.

3. Preheat ungreased heavy skillet or griddle over medium-high heat. Cook tortillas 2 to 3 minutes on each side or until bubbly and browned.

4. Stack cooked tortillas in tightly covered dish or wrap in foil. Serve warm. (If desired, tortillas may be made ahead for later use. Cool tortillas; wrap airtight and refrigerate. To reheat tortillas, wrap with foil and heat in 350°F oven 12 minutes.)

Makes 8 large or 12 small tortillas

orange coconut muffins

¾ cup all-purpose flour

¾ cup whole wheat flour

⅔ cup toasted wheat germ

½ cup sugar

½ cup flaked coconut

1½ teaspoons baking soda

½ teaspoon salt

1 cup sour cream

2 eggs

1 can (11 ounces) mandarin oranges, drained

½ cup chopped nuts

Preheat oven to 400°F. Butter 12 (2½-inch) muffin cups.

Combine flours, wheat germ, sugar, coconut, baking soda and salt in large bowl. Blend sour cream, eggs and oranges in small bowl; stir into flour mixture just until moistened. Fold in nuts. Spoon into prepared muffin cups, filling ¾ full.

Bake 18 to 20 minutes or until wooden pick inserted in center comes out clean. Remove from pan. Cool on wire rack.   *Makes 12 muffins*

Favorite recipe from **Wisconsin Milk Marketing Board**

healthy zucchini bread

⅔ cup pitted prunes

3 tablespoons water

1 cup sugar

½ cup orange juice

1 teaspoon grated orange peel

2 cups grated zucchini (about 6 medium)

1½ cups all-purpose flour

1½ cups whole wheat flour

2 teaspoons pumpkin pie spice*

1 teaspoon baking powder

1 teaspoon baking soda

¼ teaspoon salt

¼ cup plain low-fat yogurt

*Or substitute 1 teaspoon ground cinnamon, ½ teaspoon ground ginger, ¼ teaspoon ground allspice and ¼ teaspoon ground nutmeg for 2 teaspoons pumpkin pie spice.

1. Preheat oven to 350°F. Spray 9×5-inch loaf pan with nonstick cooking spray.

2. Combine prunes and water in food processor or blender; process until smooth. Combine prune mixture, sugar, orange juice and orange peel in large bowl; mix well. Stir in zucchini.

3. Combine flours, pumpkin pie spice, baking powder, baking soda and salt in medium bowl. Stir half of flour mixture into zucchini mixture, then stir in half of yogurt. Repeat with remaining flour mixture and yogurt; stir just until blended. Pour batter into prepared pan.

4. Bake 1 hour and 15 minutes or until toothpick inserted into center of loaf comes out clean. Cool in pan 10 minutes. Remove from pan; cool completely on wire rack. For best flavor, wrap bread in plastic wrap and store overnight before serving.

Makes 12 servings

spiced brown bread muffins

2 cups whole wheat flour
⅔ cup all-purpose flour
⅔ cup packed brown sugar
2 teaspoons baking soda
1 teaspoon pumpkin pie spice*
2 cups buttermilk
¾ cup raisins

Or substitute ½ teaspoon ground cinnamon, ¼ teaspoon ground ginger and ⅛ teaspoon each ground allspice and ground nutmeg for 1 teaspoon pumpkin pie spice.

Preheat oven to 350°F. Grease 6 jumbo (4-inch) muffin cups. Combine flours, sugar, baking soda and pumpkin pie spice in large bowl. Stir in buttermilk just until flour mixture is moistened. Fold in raisins. Spoon into prepared muffin cups. Bake 35 to 40 minutes until toothpick inserted into centers comes out clean. Remove from pan.

Makes 6 jumbo muffins

grandma's® molasses banana bread

1 cup whole wheat flour
¾ cup all-purpose flour
2 teaspoons baking soda
½ teaspoon salt
½ cup butter, softened
3 large bananas, mashed
1 cup GRANDMA'S® Molasses
1 egg
½ cup chopped walnuts

Heat oven to 350°F. In medium bowl, combine flours, baking soda, and salt; set aside. Cream butter in large bowl. Beat in bananas, molasses and egg. Stir in walnuts. Mix in dry ingredients just until blended. Pour mixture into greased and floured 9×5-loaf pan. Bake 50 to 60 minutes. Cool on wire rack. *Makes 1 loaf*

spiced brown bread muffin

bread basket

Who wants ordinary white bread when there's multi-grain, oat bread, honey wheat and so much more! You'll be surprised at how easy it is to make yeast bread in these days of electric mixers, bread machines and quick-rise yeast. You'll be even more amazed at how quickly those warm slices of homemade bread disappear. Yeast bread takes a little time, but it's very satisfying. Even a less-than-perfect loaf tastes perfectly delicious.

three-grain bread

1 cup whole wheat flour
¾ cup all-purpose flour
1 package rapid-rise active dry yeast
1 cup milk
2 tablespoons honey
3 teaspoons olive oil
1 teaspoon salt
½ cup old-fashioned oats
¼ cup whole grain cornmeal
1 egg beaten with 1 tablespoon water (optional)
1 tablespoon old-fashioned oats (optional)

1. Combine whole wheat flour, all-purpose flour and yeast in large bowl. Stir milk, honey, olive oil and salt in small saucepan over low heat until warm (120° to 140°F). Stir milk mixture into flour; beat 3 minutes with electric mixer at high speed. Mix in oats and cornmeal on low speed. If dough is too wet, add additional flour by teaspoonfuls until it begins to come together.

2. To knead using stand mixer, replace paddle attachment with dough hook; beat on medium speed 5 minutes after ball of dough forms. To knead by hand, place dough on floured board and knead 8 minutes or until dough is smooth and elastic. Place dough in large lightly oiled bowl; turn once to oil surface. Cover and let dough rise in warm place about 1 hour or until dough is puffy and does not spring back when touched.

3. Punch dough down and shape into 8-inch-long loaf. Place on baking sheet lightly dusted with cornmeal or flour. Cover; let rise in warm place until almost double, about 45 minutes. Meanwhile, preheat oven to 375°F.

4. Make shallow slash down center of loaf with sharp knife. Brush lightly with egg mixture and sprinkle with oats, if desired. Bake 30 minutes or until loaf sounds hollow when tapped. Remove to wire rack to cool. *Makes 1 loaf*

wheat germ bread

¾ cup wheat germ, divided
¾ cup all-purpose flour
½ cup whole wheat flour
¼ cup packed light brown sugar
 1 teaspoon baking soda
½ teaspoon baking powder
¼ teaspoon salt
½ cup raisins
 1 cup buttermilk
¼ cup (½ stick) butter or margarine, melted
 1 egg

1. Preheat oven to 350°F. Spray 8×4-inch loaf pan with nonstick cooking spray. Set aside 2 tablespoons wheat germ.

2. Combine remaining wheat germ, all-purpose flour, whole wheat flour, sugar, baking soda, baking powder and salt in large bowl. Add raisins; stir until coated. Beat buttermilk, butter and egg in small bowl until blended. Stir into flour mixture. Pour into prepared pan; sprinkle with reserved 2 tablespoons wheat germ.

3. Bake 40 to 50 minutes or until toothpick inserted into center comes out clean. Cool in pan on wire rack 10 minutes. Remove from pan and cool 30 minutes on rack.

Makes 12 servings

wheat germ bread

good morning bread

¼ cup water

1 cup mashed ripe bananas (about 3 medium)

3 tablespoons vegetable oil

1 teaspoon salt

2¼ cups bread flour

¾ cup whole wheat flour

¾ cup chopped pitted dates

½ cup old-fashioned oats

¼ cup nonfat dry milk powder

1 teaspoon grated orange peel (optional)

1 teaspoon ground cinnamon

2 teaspoons active dry yeast

Bread Machine Directions

1. Measuring carefully, place all ingredients in bread machine pan in order specified by owner's manual.

2. Program basic cycle and desired crust setting; press start. Immediately remove baked bread from pan; cool on wire rack. Serve with desired toppings.

Makes 1 (1½-pound) loaf

Note: This recipe produces a moist, slightly dense loaf that has a lower volume than other loaves. The banana flavor is more prominent when the bread is toasted.

whole wheat herb bread

⅔ cup water

⅔ cup milk

2 teaspoons sugar

2 packages active dry yeast

3 egg whites, lightly beaten

3 tablespoons olive oil

1 teaspoon salt

½ teaspoon dried basil

½ teaspoon dried oregano

4 to 4½ cups whole wheat flour, divided

1. Bring water to a boil in small saucepan. Remove from heat; stir in milk and sugar. When mixture cools to warm (110° to 115°F), add yeast. Mix well; let stand 10 minutes or until bubbly.

2. Blend egg whites, oil, salt, basil and oregano in large bowl. Add yeast mixture; mix well. Add 4 cups flour, ½ cup at a time, mixing well after each addition, until dough is no longer sticky. Turn out onto lightly floured surface. Knead about 5 minutes, adding enough of remaining flour to make smooth and elastic dough. Form into a ball. Cover; let rise in warm place about 1 hour or until doubled in bulk.

3. Preheat oven to 350°F. Lightly spray baking sheet with nonstick cooking spray. Punch down dough and place on lightly floured surface. Divide into 4 pieces and roll each piece into a ball; place on prepared baking sheet. Bake 30 to 35 minutes or until golden brown and loaves sound hollow when tapped.

Makes 4 round loaves (6 slices per loaf)

whole wheat herb bread

honey wheat bread

½ cup water

3 tablespoons honey

1 egg

2 tablespoons butter or margarine, softened

1 teaspoon salt

2 cups all-purpose flour

¾ cup whole wheat flour

¼ cup nonfat dry milk powder

2 teaspoons active dry yeast

Bread Machine Directions

1. Measuring carefully, place all ingredients in bread machine pan in order specified by owner's manual.

2. Program basic or white cycle and desired crust setting; press start. *Do not use delay cycle.* Remove baked bread from pan; cool on wire rack.

Makes 1 (1-pound) loaf

Wheat bread rises because a protein in the flour (gluten) forms an elastic network that traps air bubbles from the yeast. Breads made from 100% whole wheat flour can be dense and heavy because the bran in whole wheat is in tiny pieces with sides sharp enough to break some strands of gluten and limit rising. That's why many bread recipes call for all-purpose flour as well as whole wheat flour.

pumpernickel

¼ cup warm water (105° to 115°F)
1 package active dry yeast
1 tablespoon sugar
1½ cups whole wheat flour
½ cup rye flour
½ cup all-purpose flour
1 tablespoon caraway seeds
1 tablespoon butter or margarine
1 teaspoon salt
½ to ¾ cup evaporated or fresh milk, at room temperature
Cold water
Melted butter or margarine (optional)

1. Combine warm water, yeast and sugar in small bowl. Let stand until bubbly, about 5 minutes.

2. Fit food processor with steel blade. Measure flours, caraway seeds, butter and salt into work bowl. Process until mixed, about 10 seconds. Add yeast mixture; process until blended, about 10 seconds.

3. Turn on processor and very slowly drizzle just enough milk through feed tube so dough forms a ball that cleans the sides of the bowl. Process until ball turns around bowl about 25 times. Turn off processor and let dough stand 1 to 2 minutes.

4. Turn on processor and gradually drizzle in enough remaining milk to make dough soft but not sticky. Process until dough turns around bowl about 15 times.

5. Shape dough into ball and place in lightly greased bowl, turning to grease all sides. Cover; let stand 15 minutes. Shape into rope about 15 inches long and place diagonally on large greased cookie sheet. Cover; let stand in warm place (85°F) until doubled, about 1 hour.

6. Heat oven to 350°F. Brush cold water over loaf. Bake 35 to 40 minutes until loaf sounds hollow when tapped. Remove from cookie sheet and cool on wire rack. Brush melted butter over warm loaf, if desired. *Makes 1 loaf*

whole wheat focaccia

1 teaspoon olive oil
1 cup chopped onion
¼ cup chopped red bell pepper
3 cloves garlic, chopped
½ teaspoon paprika
2 teaspoons vegetable oil
2 cups whole wheat flour
½ cup all-purpose flour, divided
1 package rapid-rise active dry yeast
½ teaspoon sugar
¼ teaspoon salt
1 cup warm water (120°F)
2 teaspoons dried oregano
¼ to ½ teaspoon black pepper

1. For topping, heat olive oil in large nonstick skillet over medium-low heat. Cook and stir onion, bell pepper, garlic and paprika 5 minutes or until tender. Set aside.

2. Brush 12-inch pizza pan with oil; set aside. Combine whole wheat flour, 2 tablespoons all-purpose flour, yeast, sugar and salt in large bowl. Stir in warm water until well mixed.

3. Sprinkle clean work surface with 1 tablespoon all-purpose flour. Turn out dough onto surface; knead 3 minutes or until smooth, adding up to 2 tablespoons all-purpose flour to prevent sticking if necessary. Cover with inverted bowl or clean towel; let rest 10 minutes.

4. Place oven rack in lowest position; preheat oven to 425°F. Knead dough on lightly floured surface 3 minutes or until smooth and elastic, adding remaining all-purpose flour as needed to make smooth and elastic dough. Roll out dough into 13-inch round; transfer to prepared pan. Crimp edge of dough to form rim.

5. Spread topping on dough; sprinkle with oregano and black pepper. Bake 15 to 20 minutes or until edge of crust is lightly browned. Remove from pan; cool on wire rack.
Makes 8 servings

golden apple buttermilk bread

1½ cups unsifted all-purpose flour

1 cup whole wheat flour

½ cup natural bran cereal

1 teaspoon baking soda

½ teaspoon baking powder

¼ teaspoon ground ginger

1⅓ cups buttermilk

¾ cup sugar

¼ cup vegetable oil

1 large egg

1 teaspoon grated orange peel

1 cup chopped Washington Golden Delicious apples

1. Heat oven to 350°F. Grease 9×5-inch loaf pan. In medium bowl, combine flours, cereal, baking soda, baking powder and ginger. In large bowl, beat together buttermilk, sugar, oil, egg and orange peel.

2. Add flour mixture to buttermilk mixture, stirring just until combined. Fold in apples. Spread batter in prepared pan and bake 45 to 50 minutes or until wooden toothpick inserted into center comes out clean. Cool bread in pan 10 minutes. Remove from pan and cool on wire rack.   *Makes 1 loaf (8 servings)*

Favorite recipe from **Washington Apple Commission**

golden apple buttermilk bread

chili corn bread

Nonstick cooking spray
¼ cup chopped red bell pepper
¼ cup chopped green bell pepper
2 small jalapeño peppers,* minced
2 cloves garlic, minced
¾ cup corn
1½ cups yellow whole grain cornmeal
½ cup all-purpose flour
2 tablespoons sugar
2 teaspoons baking powder
½ teaspoon baking soda
½ teaspoon ground cumin
½ teaspoon salt
1½ cups buttermilk
1 egg
2 egg whites
¼ cup (½ stick) butter, melted

Jalapeño peppers can sting and irritate the skin, so wear rubber gloves when handling peppers and do not touch your eyes.

1. Preheat oven to 425°F. Spray 8-inch square baking pan with cooking spray.

2. Spray small skillet with cooking spray. Add bell peppers, jalapeños and garlic; cook and stir 3 to 4 minutes or until peppers are tender. Stir in corn; cook 1 to 2 minutes. Remove from heat.

3. Combine cornmeal, flour, sugar, baking powder, baking soda, cumin and salt in large bowl. Add buttermilk, egg, egg whites and butter; mix until blended. Stir in corn mixture. Pour batter into prepared baking pan.

4. Bake 25 to 30 minutes or until golden brown. Cool on wire rack.

Makes 12 servings

molasses brown bread

1 cup all-purpose flour
1 cup graham or rye flour
1 cup whole wheat flour
1 teaspoon baking soda
½ teaspoon salt
1 cup buttermilk
1 cup light molasses
½ cup golden or dark raisins
½ cup chopped walnuts or pecans

1. Preheat oven to 350°F. Spray 9×5-inch loaf pan with nonstick cooking spray.

2. Combine all-purpose flour, graham flour, whole wheat flour, baking soda and salt in large bowl. Add buttermilk and molasses; mix well. Stir in raisins and nuts. Spoon batter evenly into prepared pan.

3. Bake 50 to 55 minutes or until toothpick inserted near center comes out clean. Cool in pan 10 minutes on wire rack. Turn bread out onto wire rack to cool completely. Serve at room temperature with cream cheese, if desired.

Makes about 16 (½-inch) slices

Graham flour is coarsely ground whole wheat flour. It's named after Reverend Sylvester Graham, an advocate of healthy foods back in the 1830s who created the ever-popular graham cracker. Regular whole wheat flour may be substituted.

marble swirl bread

2¾ to 3¼ cups all-purpose flour, divided
¼ cup sugar
1 package active dry yeast
1 teaspoon salt
1⅓ cups plus 1 tablespoon water
¼ cup (½ stick) butter or margarine
1 whole egg
2 tablespoons molasses
2 teaspoons unsweetened cocoa powder
1 teaspoon instant coffee powder
1 to 1¼ cups rye flour
1 egg, separated

1. Combine 1½ cups all-purpose flour, sugar, yeast and salt in large bowl; set aside.

2. Heat 1⅓ cups water and butter in small saucepan over low heat until mixture is 120° to 130°F. (Butter does not need to completely melt.) Gradually beat water mixture into flour mixture with electric mixer at low speed. Increase speed to medium; beat 2 minutes.

3. Reduce speed to low; beat in 1 egg and ½ cup all-purpose flour. Increase speed to medium; beat 2 minutes. Reserve half of batter (about 1⅓ cups) in another bowl. Stir enough remaining all-purpose flour into remaining batter to make stiff dough; set aside.

4. To make darker dough, stir molasses, cocoa, coffee powder and enough rye flour into reserved batter to make stiff dough. Cover doughs; let rise in warm place about 1 hour or until doubled in bulk.

5. Punch down doughs. Knead doughs separately on lightly floured surface 1 minute. Cover; let rest 10 minutes. Grease large baking sheet. Roll out white dough into 12×9-inch rectangle with lightly floured rolling pin; set aside.

6. Roll out rye dough into 12×8-inch rectangle; place on top of white dough. Starting with 12-inch side, roll up doughs jelly-roll style. Pinch seam and ends to

continued on page 112

marble swirl bread, continued

seal. Place loaf, seam side down, on prepared baking sheet, tucking ends under. Cover; let rise in warm place about 45 minutes or until doubled in bulk.

7. Preheat oven to 350°F. Add remaining 1 tablespoon water to egg yolk; beat just until blended. Make 3 (½-inch-deep) slashes across top of loaf with sharp knife. Brush with egg yolk mixture.

8. Bake 35 to 40 minutes or until loaf is browned and sounds hollow when tapped. Immediately remove from baking sheet; cool on wire rack.   Makes 1 loaf

crusty rye bread

     1 cup water
     1 tablespoon butter or margarine, softened
     1 teaspoon salt
  2½ cups all-purpose flour
    ½ cup rye flour
    ¼ cup packed light brown sugar
  1½ teaspoons grated orange peel
     1 teaspoon caraway seeds
     2 teaspoons active dry yeast

Bread Machine Directions

1. Measuring carefully, place all ingredients in bread machine pan in order specified by owner's manual.

2. Program basic or white cycle and desired crust setting; press start. Remove baked bread from pan; cool on wire rack.   *Makes 1 (1½-pound) loaf (12 to 16 servings)*

many grains bread

2¾ to 3¼ cups all-purpose flour, divided

3 cups graham/whole wheat flour, divided

4½ teaspoons (2 packets) RED STAR® Active Dry Yeast or QUICK•RISE™ Yeast or Bread Machine Yeast

4 teaspoons salt

3 cups water

½ cup dark molasses

¼ cup vegetable oil

½ cup buckwheat flour

½ cup rye flour

½ cup soy flour

½ cup yellow cornmeal

½ cup quick rolled oats

Butter

Combine 1½ cups all-purpose flour, 2 cups graham/whole wheat flour, yeast, and salt in large bowl; mix well. Heat water, molasses, and oil together until very warm (120° to 130°F). Add to flour mixture. Blend at low speed until moistened; beat 3 minutes at medium speed. By hand, gradually stir in buckwheat, rye and soy flours, cornmeal, oats, remaining graham/whole wheat flour and enough remaining all-purpose flour to make a firm dough. Knead on floured surface 5 to 8 minutes. Place in large greased bowl, turning to grease top. Cover; let rise in warm place (about 1 hour; until until dough tests ripe* 30 minutes for Quick•Rise™ or Bread Machine Yeast).

Punch down dough. Divide into 2 parts. On lightly floured surface, shape each half into round loaf.

Place loaves on large greased baking sheet. Cover; let rise in warm place (about 40 to 45 minutes; or until indention remains after lightly touching side of loaf 30 minutes for Quick•Rise™ or Bread Machine Yeast).

Preheat oven to 375°F. With sharp knife, make a cross slash on top of each loaf. Bake 35 to 40 minutes until bread sounds hollow when tapped. If bread starts to become too dark, cover loosely with foil during last 5 to 10 minutes of baking. Remove from baking sheet. Brush with butter; cool on wire racks.   *Makes 2 round loaves*

*Stick two fingers into risen dough up to second knuckle and take out. If the indention remains, the dough is ripe and ready to punch down and shape.

savory summertime oat bread

Nonstick cooking spray
½ cup finely chopped onion
2 cups whole wheat flour
4¼ to 4½ cups all-purpose flour, divided
2 cups old-fashioned oats
¼ cup sugar
2 packages quick-rise active dry yeast
1½ teaspoons salt
1½ cups water
1¼ cups milk
¼ cup (½ stick) butter
1 cup finely shredded carrots
3 tablespoons dried parsley flakes
1 tablespoon butter, melted

1. Spray small nonstick skillet with cooking spray; heat over medium heat until hot. Cook and stir onion 3 minutes or until tender. Set aside.

2. Stir together whole wheat flour, 1 cup all-purpose flour, oats, sugar, yeast and salt in large bowl. Heat water, milk and ¼ cup butter in medium saucepan over low heat until mixture reaches 120° to 130°F. Add to flour mixture. Blend at low speed just until dry ingredients are moistened; beat 3 minutes at medium speed. Stir in carrots, onion, parsley and remaining 3¼ to 3½ cups all-purpose flour until dough is no longer sticky.

3. Knead dough on lightly floured surface 5 to 8 minutes or until smooth and elastic. Place in large bowl lightly sprayed with cooking spray; turn dough over to coat. Cover and let rise in warm place about 30 minutes or until doubled in bulk. Punch dough down. Cover and let rest 10 minutes.

4. Spray two 8×4-inch loaf pans with cooking spray. Shape dough into 2 loaves; place in pans. Brush with melted butter. Cover; let rise in warm place 30 minutes or until doubled in bulk. Meanwhile, preheat oven to 350°F.

5. Bake 40 to 45 minutes or until bread sounds hollow when tapped. Remove from pans; cool on wire racks.   *Makes 24 servings (2 loaves)*

whole wheat loaves

3 cups whole wheat flour, divided
2¼ to 2¾ cups all-purpose flour, divided
½ cup wheat germ
2 packages active dry yeast
2 teaspoons salt
1¼ cups milk
1 cup water
⅓ cup honey
¼ cup (½ stick) butter or margarine

1. Combine 2 cups whole wheat flour, 1 cup all-purpose flour, wheat germ, yeast and salt in large bowl.

2. Combine milk, water, honey and butter in medium saucepan. Heat over low heat until mixture is 120° to 130°F. (Butter does not need to completely melt.)

3. Gradually beat milk mixture into flour mixture with electric mixer at medium speed. Reduce speed to low. Beat in remaining 1 cup whole wheat flour. Beat 2 minutes at medium speed. Stir in enough additional all-purpose flour, about 1¼ cups, to make soft dough.

4. Turn out dough onto lightly floured surface. Knead 8 to 10 minutes, adding enough remaining ½ cup all-purpose flour to make smooth and elastic dough.

5. Shape dough into a ball; place in large greased bowl. Turn once to grease surface. Cover; let rise in warm place about 1 hour or until doubled in bulk.

6. Punch down dough. Knead dough on lightly floured surface 1 minute. Cut dough into halves. Cover; let rest 10 minutes. Grease two 8×4-inch loaf pans

7. Roll out each half of dough into 12×8-inch rectangle with lightly floured rolling pin. Starting with 8-inch side, roll up dough jelly-roll style. Pinch seam to seal. Place loaves, seam side down, in prepared pans, tucking ends under. Cover; let rise in warm place about 45 minutes or until doubled in bulk.

8. Meanwhile, preheat oven to 350°F. Bake 30 to 35 minutes or until loaves sound hollow when tapped. Remove from pans; cool on wire racks.

Makes 24 servings (2 loaves)

whole wheat loaf

boston brown bread

½ cup rye flour
½ cup yellow cornmeal
½ cup whole wheat flour
3 tablespoons sugar
1 teaspoon baking soda
¾ teaspoon salt
½ cup chopped walnuts
½ cup raisins
1 cup buttermilk
⅓ cup molasses
Boiling water

1. Generously grease 3 (16-ounce) vegetable cans and 1 side of 3 (6-inch) square foil pieces with shortening.

2. Combine rye flour, cornmeal, whole wheat flour, sugar, baking soda and salt in large bowl. Stir in walnuts and raisins. Whisk buttermilk and molasses in medium bowl until smooth. Add buttermilk mixture to dry ingredients; stir until well mixed.

3. Spoon mixture evenly into prepared cans. Place 1 piece of foil, greased side down, on top of each can. Secure foil with rubber bands or cotton string. Place filled cans in deep 4-quart saucepan or Dutch oven.* Pour boiling water around cans so water comes halfway up sides of cans. (Make sure foil tops do not touch boiling water.)

4. Bring to a boil over high heat. Reduce heat to low. Cover; simmer (water should be bubbling very slowly) 1¼ to 1½ hours or until wooden skewer inserted in center of bread comes out clean. Remove cans from saucepan. Immediately run knife around inside edges of cans to loosen breads. Invert and gently shake breads out of cans. Cool completely on wire rack. *Makes 3 loaves*

*To bake loaves instead of steam, preheat oven to 325°F. Prepare batter as directed in steps 1 through 3 and spoon into prepared cans. Do not cover with foil. Bake 45 to 50 minutes or until tops are brown and wooden skewer inserted in center comes out clean. Immediately run knife around inside edges of cans. Invert and gently shake breads out of cans. Cool completely on wire rack. Makes 3 loaves.

wild rice three grain bread

1 package active dry yeast
⅓ cup warm water (105° to 115°F)
2 cups milk, scalded and cooled to 105° to 115°F
½ cup honey
2 tablespoons butter, melted
2 teaspoons salt
4 to 4½ cups bread flour or unbleached all-purpose flour
2 cups whole wheat flour
½ cup rye flour
½ cup uncooked rolled oats
1 cup cooked wild rice
1 egg, beaten with 1 tablespoon water
½ cup hulled sunflower seeds

In large bowl, dissolve yeast in water. Add milk, honey, butter and salt. Stir in 2 cups bread flour, whole wheat flour, rye flour and oats to make a soft dough. Add wild rice; cover and let rest 15 minutes. Stir in enough additional bread flour to make a stiff dough. Turn dough out onto board and knead 10 minutes. Add more flour as necessary to keep dough from sticking. Turn dough into lightly greased bowl; turn dough over to coat. Cover and let rise until doubled, about 2 hours. Punch down dough. Knead briefly on lightly oiled board. To shape dough, divide into 3 portions; roll into long strands. Braid strands and place on greased baking sheet in wreath shape, or divide in half and place each half in greased 9½×5½-inch loaf pans. Let rise until doubled, about 45 minutes. Brush tops of loaves with egg mixture; slash loaves if desired. Sprinkle with sunflower seeds. Bake at 375°F 45 minutes or until loaves sound hollow when tapped. *Makes 1 braided wreath or 2 loaves*

Favorite recipe from **Minnesota Cultivated Wild Rice Council**

onion buckwheat bread

1 pound diced white onions

3 tablespoons olive oil

4½ teaspoons active dry yeast

1½ cups warm water, at 90°F

½ cup milk

6½ cups unbleached bread flour

½ cup buckwheat flour

5 teaspoons sea salt

1 tablespoon finely chopped fresh rosemary

¾ cup (3 ounces) shredded Gouda or Cheddar cheese

Unbleached bread flour as needed for kneading

4 tablespoons poppy seeds or nigella seeds (onion seeds)

1. Sauté onions in olive oil in large skillet over medium-high heat until just browned, about 5 minutes. Set aside to cool.

2. Combine yeast with water in large bowl; let sit 10 minutes until bubbly.

3. Add milk to yeast mixture and stir to combine.

4. Gradually add bread flour, buckwheat flour, salt, rosemary and onions to yeast mixture.

5. When mixture is well combined, add cheese and blend. The dough will be slightly sticky.

6. Knead dough on lightly floured surface about 10 minutes, until smooth and elastic. Add additional bread flour as needed if dough is too soft.

7. Lightly oil clean bowl. Place dough in bowl; cover and let rise until doubled in bulk, 1½ to 2 hours.

8. Gently punch down dough and place on lightly floured surface. Cut dough in half and shape into round loaves. Spritz top of each loaf with water, and press on poppy seeds or nigella seeds. Place on lightly floured baking sheet; cover and let rise until almost doubled in bulk, 45 minutes to 1 hour.

continued on page 124

onion buckwheat bread

onion buckwheat bread, continued

9. Preheat oven to 450°F. Slash tops of loaves with knife and place in oven. Add steam by placing 2 ice cubes in pan on bottom of oven. Bake 10 minutes. *Reduce heat to 400°F* and bake an additional 35 to 40 minutes. Cool loaves completely on rack. *Makes 2 (10-inch) round loaves*

Favorite recipe from **National Onion Association**

honey whole-grain bread

 3 cups whole wheat flour, divided
 2 cups warm (110°F) whole milk
 ¾ to 1 cup all-purpose flour, divided
 ¼ cup honey
 2 tablespoons vegetable oil
 1 package active dry yeast
 ¾ teaspoon salt

Slow Cooker Directions

1. Spray 1-quart casserole, soufflé dish or other high-sided baking pan that fits into slow cooker with nonstick cooking spray. Combine 1½ cups whole wheat flour, milk, ½ cup all-purpose flour, honey, oil, yeast and salt in large bowl. Beat with electric mixer at medium speed 2 minutes.

2. Add remaining 1½ cups whole wheat flour and ¼ to ½ cup all-purpose flour until dough is no longer sticky. (If mixer has difficulty mixing dough, mix in remaining flours with wooden spoon.) Transfer to prepared dish.

3. Make foil handles with strips of heavy-duty foil. Criss cross 3 or 4 strips and place in slow cooker. Place dish on strips in slow cooker. Cover; cook on HIGH 3 hours or until edges are browned.

4. Use foil handles to lift dish from slow cooker. Let stand 5 minutes. Unmold on wire rack to cool. *Makes 8 to 10 servings*

whole grain main

Making your main course a grain course opens up a whole world of wonderful options. Dishes such as Thin-Crust Whole Wheat Veggie Pizza and Hoppin' Shrimp and Brown Rice are just two of the family-pleasing options. Grain is so versatile it's an important part of every ethnic cuisine from Mediterranean to Asian. Adding whole grain pasta or bulgur wheat to a weeknight dinner is as easy as having it available in your pantry.

hoppin' shrimp and brown rice

1 bag boil-in-bag instant brown rice
  Nonstick cooking spray
2 cups black-eyed peas
2 cups reduced-sodium vegetable broth
2 cups salsa
1 can (14½ ounces) no-salt-added diced tomatoes
1 bag (12 ounces) cooked baby shrimp
1 box (10 ounces) frozen whole okra
4 stalks celery, chopped
¼ cup chopped red onion
¼ cup chopped cilantro
  Juice of ½ lime
½ teaspoon black pepper

1. Prepare rice according to package directions; keep warm.

2. Spray large skillet with cooking spray. Add black-eyed peas, broth, salsa, tomatoes, shrimp, okra, celery, onion, cilantro, lime juice and black pepper. Simmer over medium-high heat 20 minutes or until heated through, stirring occasionally.

3. Serve with rice and additional salsa, lime wedge and cilantro if desired.

Makes 4 servings

Apricot Cole Slaw: If desired, serve with Apricot Cole Slaw. Whisk ¼ cup balsamic vinegar, 2 tablespoons extra-virgin olive oil, ¼ cup apricot fruit spread, ¼ cup chopped fresh basil, ½ teaspoon minced garlic and ¼ teaspoon black pepper in large bowl. Toss with 3 cups cole slaw mix.

asian pesto noodles

1 pound large raw shrimp, peeled and deveined
   Spicy Asian Pesto (recipe follows)
12 ounces uncooked soba (buckwheat) noodles

1. Marinate shrimp in ¾ cup pesto.

2. Cook soba noodles according to package directions; drain and set aside. Preheat broiler or grill.

3. Place marinated shrimp on metal skewers. (If using wooden skewers, soak in water 30 minutes to prevent burning.) Place skewers under broiler or on grill; cook until shrimp are opaque, about 3 minutes per side.

4. To serve, toss soba noodles with remaining pesto. Serve with shrimp skewers.

Makes 4 servings

spicy asian pesto

3 cups fresh basil leaves
3 cups fresh cilantro leaves
3 cups fresh mint leaves
¾ cup peanut oil
3 tablespoons sugar
2 to 3 tablespoons lime juice
5 cloves garlic, chopped
2 teaspoons fish sauce *or* 1 teaspoon salt
1 serrano pepper,* finely chopped

Serrano peppers can sting and irritate the skin, so wear rubber gloves when handling peppers and do not touch your eyes.

Combine all pesto ingredients in blender or food processor; blend until smooth.

Makes 2½ cups

whole wheat penne with broccoli and sausage

6 to 7 ounces (about ½ package) whole wheat penne pasta

8 ounces broccoli florets

8 ounces mild Italian turkey sausage, casings removed

1 medium onion, quartered and sliced

2 cloves garlic, minced

2 teaspoons grated lemon peel

¼ teaspoon salt

⅛ teaspoon black pepper

⅓ cup grated Parmesan cheese

1. Cook pasta according to package directions, adding broccoli during last 5 to 6 minutes of cooking. Drain; return to pan and keep warm.

2. Meanwhile, heat large skillet over medium heat. Crumble sausage into skillet. Add onion; cook until sausage is brown, stirring to break up meat. Drain fat.

3. Add garlic; cook and stir 1 minute over medium heat. Add sausage mixture, lemon peel, salt and pepper to pasta; toss until blended. Add cheese; toss until cheese is melted. *Makes 6 (1⅓-cup) servings*

Substituting whole grain pasta for regular pasta is one of the easiest ways to add nutritious whole grains to your diet. You can choose from a wide variety including pasta fortified with vitamins, as well as pasta made with spelt, soy and other grains. The hearty flavor of whole grain pasta stands up to even the most robust sauce.

whole wheat penne with broccoli and sausage

south-of-the-border lunch express

½ cup chopped seeded tomato

¼ cup chunky salsa

¼ cup rinsed and drained canned black beans

¼ cup frozen corn, thawed

1 teaspoon chopped fresh cilantro

¼ teaspoon chopped garlic

   Dash ground red pepper

1 cup cooked brown rice

   Reduced-fat Cheddar cheese (optional)

Microwave Directions

1. Combine tomato, salsa, beans, corn, cilantro, garlic and red pepper in 1-quart microwavable bowl. Cover with vented plastic wrap. Microwave on HIGH 1 to 1½ minutes or until heated through; stir.

2. Microwave rice at HIGH 1 to 1½ minutes in separate 1-quart microwavable dish or until heated through. Top with tomato mixture and cheese, if desired.

Makes 1 serving

Rice is usually categorized by the length of its grain— long, short or medium. All rice contains two forms of starch: amylose which is not sticky and amylopectin which is. Long grain rice cooks up fluffy because it has more amylose. Short- and medium-grain rices contain a larger proportion of the sticky starch (amylopectin), so the grains tend to stick together after cooking.

ham, barley and almond bake

½ cup slivered almonds

1 tablespoon butter or margarine

1 cup uncooked pearl barley

1 cup chopped carrots

1 bunch green onions, sliced

2 stalks celery, sliced

3 cloves garlic, minced

1 pound lean smoked ham, cubed

2 teaspoons dried basil

1 teaspoon dried oregano

¼ teaspoon black pepper

2 cans (14 ounces each) reduced-sodium beef broth

½ pound fresh green beans, cut into 1-inch pieces

1. Preheat oven to 350°F. Spray 13×9-inch baking dish with nonstick cooking spray.

2. Spread almonds in single layer on baking sheet. Bake 5 minutes or until golden brown, stirring frequently.

3. Melt butter in large skillet over medium-high heat. Add barley, carrots, onions, celery and garlic; cook and stir 2 minutes or until onions are tender. Remove from heat. Stir in ham, toasted almonds, basil, oregano and pepper. Spoon into prepared dish.

4. Bring broth to a boil in medium saucepan over high heat. Pour over barley mixture.

5. Cover tightly with foil; bake 20 minutes. Remove from oven; stir in green beans. Bake, covered, 30 minutes or until barley is tender.   *Makes 8 servings*

thin-crust whole wheat veggie pizza

¾ to 1 cup all-purpose flour, divided

½ cup whole wheat flour

1 teaspoon quick-rise active dry yeast

1½ teaspoons dried basil, divided

¼ teaspoon salt

1 tablespoon olive oil

1 clove garlic, minced

½ cup very warm water (120° to 130°F)

1 teaspoon yellow cornmeal

½ cup no-salt-added tomato sauce

1 cup thinly sliced mushrooms

1 large roasted red bell pepper,* cut lengthwise into thin strips *or* ¾ cup
  sliced, drained, bottled roasted red peppers

½ cup thinly sliced zucchini

⅓ cup chopped green onions

1 cup (4 ounces) shredded part-skim mozzarella cheese

¼ teaspoon red pepper flakes

*To roast pepper, cut pepper lengthwise into halves; remove stem, membrane and seeds. Broil 3 inches from heat, skin side up, until skin is blackened and blistered. Place halves in small resealable food storage bag. Seal; set aside 15 minutes. Remove pepper from bag. Peel off skin; drain on paper towel.

1. Combine ½ cup all-purpose flour, whole wheat flour, yeast, 1 teaspoon basil and salt. Blend oil with garlic in small cup; stir into flour mixture with water. Stir in ¼ cup all-purpose flour until soft, slightly sticky dough forms. Knead dough on lightly floured surface about 5 minutes, adding remaining ¼ cup all-purpose flour to make smooth and elastic dough. Shape dough into a ball. Cover; let rest 10 minutes.

2. Place oven rack in lowest position; preheat oven to 400°F. Spray 12-inch pizza pan or baking sheet with nonstick cooking spray; sprinkle with cornmeal. Roll dough into large circle on lightly floured surface. Transfer to prepared pan, stretching dough out to edge of pan.

3. Combine tomato sauce and remaining ½ teaspoon basil in small bowl; spread over crust. Top with vegetables and mozzarella; sprinkle with red pepper flakes. Bake 20 to 25 minutes or until crust is golden brown.   *Makes 4 servings*

thin-crust whole wheat veggie pizza

seasoned chicken with beans and rice

1 teaspoon vegetable oil
½ cup chopped green onions
1 teaspoon minced garlic
1½ cups reduced-sodium chicken broth
2 tablespoons all-purpose flour
3 cups frozen mixed vegetables
1 can (about 15 ounces) kidney beans, rinsed and drained
1 cup shredded cooked chicken
1 teaspoon dried rosemary
½ teaspoon dried thyme
⅛ teaspoon ground red pepper
2 cups cooked brown rice

1. Heat oil in large nonstick skillet over medium heat. Add green onions and garlic; cook 1 minute.

2. Whisk broth and flour together in medium bowl; add mixture to skillet. Add frozen vegetables, beans, chicken, rosemary, thyme and red pepper. Bring to a boil; reduce heat and simmer, covered, 6 minutes or until vegetables are tender. Serve over hot cooked brown rice. *Makes 4 servings*

Brown rice is simply white rice that hasn't been polished to remove the outer bran coating. This makes it more nutritious since a lot of B vitamins, iron and fiber are lost in the processing. You can purchase brown rice versions of basmati and jasmine rice as well as traditional long and short grain.

bulgur pilaf with tomato and zucchini

1 cup uncooked bulgur wheat

1 tablespoon olive oil

¾ cup chopped onion

2 cloves garlic, minced

½ pound zucchini (2 small), thinly sliced

1 can (14½ ounces) no-salt-added whole tomatoes, drained and coarsely chopped

1 cup reduced-sodium chicken broth

1 teaspoon dried basil

⅛ teaspoon black pepper

1. Rinse bulgur thoroughly in colander under cold water, removing any debris. Drain well; set aside.

2. Heat oil in large saucepan over medium heat. Add onion and garlic; cook and stir 3 minutes or until onion is tender. Stir in zucchini and tomatoes; reduce heat to medium-low. Cook, covered, 15 minutes or until zucchini is almost tender, stirring occasionally.

3. Stir chicken broth, bulgur, basil and pepper into vegetable mixture. Bring to a boil over high heat. Reduce heat to low. Cook, covered, over low heat 15 minutes or until bulgur is tender and liquid is almost completely absorbed, stirring occasionally. Remove from heat; let stand, covered, 10 minutes. Stir gently before serving.

Makes 8 servings

bulgur pilaf with tomato and zucchini

middle eastern turkey meatballs with couscous

  Nonstick cooking spray
1 cup finely chopped onion, divided
1 cup reduced-sodium chicken broth
⅔ cup uncooked whole wheat couscous
½ teaspoon salt, divided
1 cup baby spinach
¾ pound lean ground turkey
¼ cup egg substitute
1 tablespoon steak sauce
¾ teaspoon ground cinnamon
¾ teaspoon ground cumin
¼ teaspoon black pepper
½ cup water
2 tablespoons tomato paste

1. Spray large skillet with cooking spray; heat over medium heat. Add ¾ cup onion; cook and stir 4 minutes or until tender.

2. Bring broth to a boil in small saucepan over high heat; stir in couscous and ¼ teaspoon salt. Cover; remove from heat. Let stand 5 minutes. Stir in cooked onion and spinach; set aside.

3. Meanwhile, combine turkey, egg substitute, remaining ¼ cup onion, steak sauce, cinnamon, cumin, remaining ¼ teaspoon salt and black pepper in medium bowl; mix well. Shape into 24 (1-inch) balls.

4. Spray skillet with cooking spray; heat over medium-high heat. Add meatballs; cook about 7 minutes or until no longer pink in center, turning frequently to brown on all sides. Remove and keep warm.

5. Add water and tomato paste to skillet; whisk until blended. Bring to a boil; reduce heat to low. Add meatballs; cook until meatballs are hot.

6. Serve meatballs and sauce over couscous mixture. *Makes 4 servings*

quick oriental feast

1 bag SUCCESS® Brown Rice
Vegetable cooking spray
½ pound skinless, boneless chicken breasts, cut into strips
2 cups sliced fresh mushrooms
1 package (10 ounces) frozen pea pods, thawed and drained
1 can (8 ounces) sliced water chestnuts, drained
6 green onions, chopped
2 teaspoons cornstarch
½ cup reduced-sodium chicken broth
2 teaspoons reduced-sodium soy sauce (optional)

Prepare rice according to package directions.

Spray large skillet with cooking spray. Add chicken; stir-fry over medium-high heat until chicken is no longer pink in center. Remove chicken from skillet; set aside. Spray skillet again with cooking spray. Add mushrooms, pea pods, water chestnuts and onions; stir-fry until tender. Combine cornstarch, chicken broth and soy sauce in small bowl; mix well. Return chicken to skillet. Add cornstarch mixture; cook and stir until sauce is thickened. Serve over hot rice. *Makes 4 servings*

So many quick-cooking whole grain options are available today. There's no excuse not to choose whole wheat couscous or brown rice when they are readily available in forms that fit busy lifestyles.

italian mixed seafood

½ pound large raw shrimp, peeled and deveined
½ pound sea scallops
1 small zucchini, cut into ½-inch pieces
1 small red bell pepper, cut into ½-inch pieces
1 small red onion, cut into wedges
12 large mushrooms
1 bottle (8 ounces) Italian salad dressing
2 teaspoons dried Italian seasoning, divided
1½ cups uncooked brown rice
2 cans (about 14 ounces each) chicken broth

1. Place shrimp, scallops, zucchini, bell pepper, onion, mushrooms, salad dressing and 1 teaspoon Italian seasoning in large resealable food storage bag. Seal bag; turn to coat. Marinate in refrigerator 30 minutes, turning after 15 minutes.

2. Meanwhile, combine rice, chicken broth and remaining 1 teaspoon Italian seasoning in medium saucepan over high heat. Bring to a boil; cover and reduce heat to low. Simmer 35 minutes or until liquid is absorbed.

3. Meanwhile, prepare grill for direct cooking.

4. Drain seafood and vegetables, reserving marinade. Place seafood and vegetables in lightly oiled grill basket or on vegetable grilling grid. Grill, covered, over medium-high heat 4 to 5 minutes; turn and baste with marinade. Grill 4 to 5 minutes or until shrimp are opaque. Serve seafood and vegetables over rice.

Makes 4 to 6 servings

italian mixed seafood

cherry pork wrap

3 cups pitted Northwest fresh sweet cherries, divided

2 tablespoons chopped fresh basil

2 tablespoons finely chopped Anaheim pepper

2 teaspoons grated fresh ginger, divided

¼ teaspoon salt

12 ounces lean boneless pork loin or skinned chicken breasts, cut into 2-inch strips

½ teaspoon garlic salt

⅛ teaspoon black pepper

1 tablespoon vegetable oil

2 cups cooked brown rice*

8 flour tortillas

2 cups finely shredded romaine lettuce

Three-fourths cup uncooked brown rice, cooked in water or chicken broth according to package directions, equals about 2 cups cooked.

Chop 2 cups cherries in food processor. Combine chopped cherries, basil, Anaheim pepper, 1 teaspoon ginger and salt in large bowl; set aside. In skillet, sauté pork, remaining 1 cup pitted cherries, remaining 1 teaspoon ginger, garlic salt and black pepper in oil until pork is no longer pink; fold pork mixture into cooked rice. Wrap tortillas tightly in heavy foil; heat 10 to 15 minutes at 350°F. Portion ¼ cup *each* rice mixture, lettuce and chopped cherry mixture on one half of each tortilla. Fold in sides and roll into a bundle.   *Makes 4 servings (2 wraps per serving)*

Favorite recipe from **Northwest Cherry Growers**

soba stir-fry

8 ounces uncooked soba (buckwheat) noodles
1 tablespoon olive oil
2 cups sliced fresh shiitake mushrooms
1 medium red bell pepper, cut into thin strips
2 whole dried red chiles *or* **¼ teaspoon red pepper flakes**
1 clove garlic, minced
2 cups shredded napa cabbage
½ cup reduced-sodium vegetable broth
2 tablespoons soy sauce
1 tablespoon rice wine or dry sherry
2 teaspoons cornstarch
1 package (14 ounces) firm tofu, drained and cut into 1-inch cubes
2 green onions, thinly sliced

1. Cook noodles according to package directions, omitting salt. Drain and set aside.

2. Heat oil in large nonstick skillet or wok over medium heat. Add mushrooms, bell pepper, dried chiles and garlic. Cook 3 minutes or until mushrooms are tender.

3. Add cabbage. Cover; cook 2 minutes or until cabbage is wilted.

4. Combine chicken broth, soy sauce, rice wine and cornstarch in small bowl. Stir sauce into vegetable mixture. Cook 2 minutes or until sauce is bubbly.

5. Stir in tofu and noodles; toss gently until heated through. Sprinkle with green onions. Serve immediately. *Makes 4 servings*

whole wheat spaghetti with cauliflower and feta

3 tablespoons olive oil

1 onion, chopped

4 cloves garlic, minced

1 head cauliflower, cut into bite-sized florets

1 teaspoon salt

½ teaspoon black pepper

⅔ cup white wine or water

½ package (about 6 ounces) uncooked whole wheat spaghetti

1 pint grape tomatoes, cut into halves

½ cup coarsely chopped walnuts

¼ teaspoon crushed red pepper (optional)

½ cup crumbled feta cheese

1. Heat oil in large skillet over medium heat. Add onion; cook and stir 3 minutes until wilted. Add garlic; cook and stir 2 minutes. Add cauliflower to skillet; cook and stir 5 minutes. Season with salt and black pepper; add wine. Cover and cook about 15 minutes or until cauliflower is fork tender.

2. Meanwhile, cook pasta according to package directions. Drain and keep warm; reserve ½ cup pasta cooking water.

3. Add tomatoes, walnuts and reserved pasta water to skillet; season with red pepper, if desired. Cook 2 to 3 minutes or until tomatoes begin to soften.

4. Toss spaghetti with vegetable sauce in skillet or serving bowl; top with feta.

Makes 4 to 6 servings

whole wheat spaghetti with cauliflower and feta

barley, bean and corn frittata

2 cups water

½ cup uncooked pearl barley

¾ teaspoon salt, divided

2 teaspoons olive oil

1 can (about 15 ounces) black beans, rinsed and drained

2 cups (8 ounces) shredded Cheddar cheese, divided

¾ cup corn

½ cup chopped green bell pepper

¼ cup chopped fresh cilantro

7 eggs *or* 1¾ cups egg substitute

1 cup cottage cheese

½ teaspoon ground red pepper

1 cup medium salsa

   Sour cream (optional)

1. Bring water to a boil in medium saucepan over high heat. Add barley and ¼ teaspoon salt. Reduce heat to low. Cover and simmer 40 to 45 minutes or until tender. Remove from heat. Let stand, covered, 5 minutes. Drain.

2. Preheat oven to 400°F. Brush 10-inch cast iron or ovenproof skillet with olive oil. Layer barley, beans, 1 cup Cheddar cheese, corn, bell pepper and cilantro in skillet. Blend eggs, cottage cheese, remaining ½ teaspoon salt and ground red pepper in blender or food processor just until smooth. Carefully pour egg mixture over layers.

3. Bake 30 minutes or until egg mixture is set. Sprinkle with remaining 1 cup Cheddar cheese. Bake 5 minutes or until cheese is melted. Spoon salsa evenly over top. Let stand 5 minutes before cutting into wedges. Serve with sour cream.

Makes 6 to 8 servings

chinese-style fried brown rice

3½ cups water

2 cups uncooked long-grain brown rice

3 tablespoons vegetable oil, divided

2 eggs, lightly beaten

1 medium yellow onion, coarsely chopped

1 slice (8 ounces) smoked or baked ham, cut into thin strips

1 cup frozen green peas, thawed

1 to 2 tablespoons soy sauce

1 tablespoon dark sesame oil

Fresh cilantro (optional)

1. Combine water and rice in large saucepan. Cover and bring to a boil over high heat. Reduce heat to low and simmer 40 to 45 minutes or until rice is tender and all water is absorbed, stirring occasionally. Remove from heat and let stand, covered, 10 minutes.

2. Fluff rice with fork and spread out on greased baking sheet. Cool to room temperature, about 30 to 40 minutes, or refrigerate overnight.

3. Heat wok over medium heat about 30 seconds or until hot. Drizzle 1 tablespoon vegetable oil into wok and heat 15 seconds. Add eggs and cook 1 minute or just until set on bottom. Turn eggs over and stir to scramble until cooked but not dry. Remove eggs to bowl; set aside.

4. Add remaining 2 tablespoons vegetable oil to wok and heat 30 seconds or until hot. Add onion; stir-fry over medium-high heat about 3 minutes or until tender. Add ham strips; stir-fry 1 minute. Add cooked rice, peas, soy sauce and sesame oil; cook 5 minutes, stirring frequently. Stir in eggs and cook until heated through. Transfer to warm serving dish. Garnish with cilantro. Serve immediately.   *Makes 6 servings*

turkey breast with barley-cranberry stuffing

2 cups reduced-sodium chicken broth

1 cup uncooked quick-cooking barley

½ cup chopped onion

½ cup dried cranberries

2 tablespoons slivered almonds, toasted

½ teaspoon rubbed sage

½ teaspoon garlic-pepper seasoning

Nonstick cooking spray

1 fresh or thawed frozen bone-in turkey breast half (about 2 pounds), skinned

⅓ cup finely chopped fresh parsley

Slow Cooker Directions

1. Combine broth, barley, onion, cranberries, almonds, sage and garlic-pepper seasoning in slow cooker.

2. Spray large nonstick skillet with cooking spray; heat over medium heat. Brown turkey breast on all sides; add to slow cooker. Cover; cook on LOW 4 to 6 hours.

3. Transfer turkey to cutting board; cover with foil and let stand 10 to 15 minutes before carving. Stir parsley into sauce mixture in slow cooker. Serve sliced turkey with sauce and stuffing. *Makes 6 servings*

turkey breast with barley-cranberry stuffing

cheesy baked barley

   2 cups water
   ½ cup medium pearl barley
   ½ teaspoon salt, divided
      Nonstick cooking spray
   ½ cup diced onion
   ½ cup diced zucchini
   ½ cup diced red bell pepper
  1½ teaspoons all-purpose flour
   ¾ cup milk
   1 cup (4 ounces) shredded Italian blend cheese, divided
   1 tablespoon Dijon mustard
      Black pepper

1. Bring water to a boil in small saucepan. Add barley and ¼ teaspoon salt. Cover; reduce heat and simmer 45 minutes or until barley is tender and water is absorbed. Remove from heat. Let stand, covered, 5 minutes.

2. Preheat oven to 375°F. Spray medium skillet with cooking spray. Cook onion, zucchini and bell pepper over medium-low heat about 10 minutes or until soft. Stir in flour and remaining ¼ teaspoon salt; cook 1 to 2 minutes. Add milk, stirring constantly; cook and stir until slightly thickened. Remove from heat. Add barley, ¾ cup cheese and mustard; stir until cheese is melted. Season with pepper.

3. Spread in even layer in casserole. Sprinkle with remaining ¼ cup cheese. Bake 20 minutes or until hot. Preheat broiler. Broil casserole 1 to 2 minutes or until cheese is lightly browned. *Makes 2 servings*

beyond wheat

When you think of grain, you probably think of wheat. Well, here's another thought: It's time to try something different. Quinoa is a protein-packed grain that cooks up quickly and tastes light and delicate. If you like white rice, chances are you'll enjoy less-processed, healthier brown rice. Don't forget wild rice for a nutty change of pace. There's barley, millet and polenta, too. Maybe it's time to stop reading and start cooking?

quinoa with roasted vegetables

Nonstick cooking spray
2 medium sweet potatoes, cut into ½-inch-thick slices
1 medium eggplant, peeled, cut into ½-inch cubes
1 medium tomato, cut into wedges
1 large green bell pepper, sliced
1 small onion, cut into wedges
½ teaspoon salt
¼ teaspoon black pepper
¼ teaspoon ground red pepper
1 cup uncooked quinoa
2 cloves garlic, minced
½ teaspoon dried thyme
¼ teaspoon dried marjoram
2 cups water or reduced-sodium chicken broth

1. Preheat oven to 450°F. Line large jelly-roll pan with foil; coat with cooking spray. Arrange sweet potatoes, eggplant, tomato, bell pepper and onion on pan; coat lightly with cooking spray. Sprinkle with salt, black pepper and ground red pepper; toss to coat. Bake 20 to 30 minutes or until vegetables are browned and tender.

2. Meanwhile, place quinoa in strainer; rinse well. Coat medium saucepan with cooking spray; heat over medium heat. Add garlic, thyme and marjoram; cook and stir 1 to 2 minutes. Add quinoa; cook and stir 2 to 3 minutes. Stir in water; bring to a boil over high heat. Reduce heat to low. Simmer, covered, 15 to 20 minutes or until water is absorbed. (The quinoa will appear somewhat translucent.) Transfer quinoa to large bowl; gently mix in vegetables.

Makes 6 servings

barley beef stroganoff

2½ cups reduced-sodium vegetable broth or water

⅔ cup uncooked pearl barley (not quick-cooking)

1 package (6 ounces) sliced fresh mushrooms

½ teaspoon dried marjoram

½ teaspoon black pepper

½ pound ground beef

½ cup chopped celery

½ cup minced green onions

¼ cup fat-free half-and-half

Minced fresh parsley (optional)

Slow Cooker Directions

1. Place broth, barley, mushrooms, marjoram and pepper in slow cooker. Cover; cook on LOW 6 to 7 hours.

2. Brown beef in large nonstick skillet 6 to 8 minutes over medium-high heat, stirring to break up meat. Drain fat. Add celery and green onions; cook and stir 3 minutes. Stir beef mixture and half-and-half into slow cooker mixture. Cover; cook on HIGH 10 to 15 minutes or until beef is hot and vegetables are tender. Garnish with parsley.

Makes 4 servings

Barley is a versatile grain with a chewy texture and a mild, slightly sweet taste. Pearl barley, which is the most readily available, has been processed to strip off the hull. While this means that it is not, strictly speaking, a whole grain, pearl barley retains much of its fiber, vitamins and minerals. For an even more nutritious form of barley, look for hulled barley in health food stores.

easy cheesy ham and veggie rice casserole

1 bag boil-in-bag brown rice
2 cups broccoli florets
1 cup matchstick-size carrots
6 ounces lean ham, diced
2 ounces Swiss cheese, diced
3 ounces sharp Cheddar cheese, shredded
1 tablespoon butter or margarine
⅛ teaspoon ground red pepper

1. Cook rice in large saucepan according to package directions. Remove rice packet when cooked. Add broccoli and carrots to water; bring to a boil. Reduce heat; cover and simmer 3 minutes or until broccoli is crisp-tender.

2. Drain vegetables and return to saucepan. Stir in rice. Heat over medium-low heat. Add ham, Swiss, ¼ cup Cheddar, butter and red pepper; stir gently. Sprinkle evenly with remaining Cheddar; cover and let stand 3 minutes or until cheese melts.

Makes 4 (1½-cup) servings

brown rice with vegetables and tomato pesto

½ cup Tomato Pesto (page 168)
4 tablespoons olive oil, divided
1 medium onion, chopped
3 cloves garlic, minced
1½ cups uncooked long grain brown rice
3 cups chicken broth
2 carrots, sliced
5 ounces fresh green beans, cut into 2-inch pieces (about 1 cup)
1 cup diced yellow summer squash
1 cup broccoli florets

1. Prepare Tomato Pesto; set aside.

2. Heat 1 tablespoon oil in medium saucepan over medium-high heat. Add onion and garlic; cook and stir 3 minutes. Add rice; cook and stir 2 minutes. Gradually add chicken broth. Bring to a boil over medium-high heat. Reduce heat to low; simmer, covered, 45 minutes or until rice is tender and liquid is absorbed.

3. Heat remaining 3 tablespoons oil in large skillet over medium heat. Add carrots and beans; cook and stir 4 minutes. Add squash and broccoli; cook and stir 5 to 7 minutes until vegetables are crisp-tender.

4. Combine rice mixture and vegetable mixture in large bowl. Gently toss with Tomato Pesto.   *Makes 10 side-dish servings*

continued on page 168

brown rice with vegetables and
tomato pesto

brown rice with vegetables and tomato pesto, continued

tomato pesto

1 jar (8 ounces) sun-dried tomatoes packed in oil, undrained
2 teaspoons grated lemon peel
2 cloves garlic, minced
1½ teaspoons dried oregano *or* 5 teaspoons chopped fresh oregano
½ cup freshly grated Parmesan cheese

1. Place sun-dried tomatoes with oil, lemon peel, garlic and oregano in food processor; process until almost smooth, scraping side of bowl occasionally.

2. Add cheese; process until well combined. (Remaining pesto may be covered and refrigerated up to 1 week.) *Makes 1¼ cups*

cheese bread (gluten-free)

1¾ cups water
3 eggs
3 tablespoons vegetable oil
2 cups white rice flour
1 cup brown rice flour
1½ cups (6 ounces) grated sharp Cheddar cheese
¼ cup dry milk powder
2 tablespoons sugar
1 tablespoon instant minced onion (optional)
1 tablespoon poppy seeds (optional)
3½ teaspoons xanthan gum
2¼ teaspoons (1 packet) RED STAR® Active Dry Yeast or QUICK•RISE™ Yeast or Bread Machine Yeast
1½ teaspoons celery seeds (optional)
1½ teaspoons dried dill weed (optional)
1 teaspoon salt

Bread Machine Method

Have all ingredients at room temperature. Combine water, eggs and oil; pour into baking pan.

Combine flours, cheese, milk powder, sugar, onion, poppy seeds, xanthan gum, yeast, celery seeds, dill and salt. Blend thoroughly in bowl with wire whisk or shake together in large resealing plastic food storage bag.*

Select white or basic cycle; start machine.

For bread machines with bake only cycle, select dough cycle for mixing and rising. Press stop when cycle is complete; then select the bake only cycle to complete bread.

After mixing action begins, help any unmixed ingredients into dough with rubber spatula, keeping to edges of batter to prevent interference with kneading blade.

When bake cycle is complete, remove pan from machine. Allow bread to remain in pan about 10 minutes, then invert pan and shake gently to remove bread. Cool upright on rack before slicing.

Mixer Method

In mixing bowl, combine water, eggs and oil; mix well.

Combine flours, cheese, milk powder, sugar, onion, poppy seeds, xanthan gum, yeast, celery seeds, dill and salt. Blend thoroughly in bowl with wire whisk or shake together in large resealing plastic food storage bag.*

With mixer on low speed, gradually add flour mixture to mixing bowl until well blended. Beat about 10 minutes.

Pour batter into three 5×2½-inch greased bread pans; allow to rise about 1 hour. Bake at 375°F for 45 to 60 minutes or until toothpick comes out clean when inserted in center.

When baking is complete, remove pan from oven; let bread cool 10 minutes in pans. Remove from pans and cool completely on wire rack before slicing.

Makes 3 loaves

Gluten-free flours are very fine and need to be well blended before liquid is added to them.

italian eggplant with millet and pepper stuffing

  ¼ cup uncooked millet
  2 small eggplants (about ¾ pound total)
  ¼ cup chopped red bell pepper, divided
  ¼ cup chopped green bell pepper, divided
  1 teaspoon olive oil
  1 clove garlic, minced
1½ cups reduced-sodium vegetable broth
  ½ teaspoon ground cumin
  ½ teaspoon dried oregano
  ⅛ teaspoon red pepper flakes

1. Cook and stir millet in large heavy skillet over medium heat 5 minutes or until golden. Transfer to small bowl; set aside.

2. Cut eggplants lengthwise into halves. Scoop out flesh, leaving about ¼-inch-thick shell. Reserve shells; chop eggplant flesh. Combine 1 teaspoon red bell pepper and 1 teaspoon green bell pepper in small bowl; set aside.

3. Heat oil in same skillet over medium heat. Add chopped eggplant, remaining red and green bell pepper and garlic; cook and stir about 8 minutes or until eggplant is tender.

4. Stir in toasted millet, chicken broth, cumin, oregano and red pepper flakes. Bring to a boil over high heat. Reduce heat to medium-low. Simmer, covered, 35 minutes or until all liquid has been absorbed and millet is tender. Remove from heat; let stand, covered, 10 minutes. Preheat oven to 350°F. Pour 1 cup water into 8-inch square baking pan.

5. Fill reserved eggplant shells with eggplant-millet mixture. Sprinkle shells with reserved chopped bell peppers, pressing in lightly. Carefully place filled shells in prepared pan. Bake 15 minutes or until heated through.   *Makes 4 servings*

italian eggplant with millet and
pepper stuffing

polenta lasagna

4¼ cups water, divided
1½ cups whole grain yellow cornmeal
4 teaspoons finely chopped fresh marjoram
1 teaspoon olive oil
1 pound fresh mushrooms, sliced
1 cup chopped leeks
1 clove garlic, minced
½ cup (2 ounces) shredded part-skim mozzarella cheese
2 tablespoons chopped fresh basil
1 tablespoon chopped fresh oregano
⅛ teaspoon black pepper
2 medium red bell peppers, chopped
¼ cup freshly grated Parmesan cheese, divided

1. Bring 4 cups water to a boil in medium saucepan over high heat. Slowly add cornmeal to water, stirring constantly with wire whisk. Reduce heat to low; stir in marjoram. Simmer 15 to 20 minutes or until polenta thickens and pulls away from side of saucepan. Spread in ungreased 13×9-inch baking pan. Cover and chill about 1 hour or until firm.

2. Heat oil in medium nonstick skillet over medium heat. Cook and stir mushrooms, leeks and garlic 5 minutes or until vegetables are crisp-tender. Stir in mozzarella, basil, oregano and black pepper.

3. Place bell peppers and remaining ¼ cup water in food processor or blender; cover and process until smooth. Preheat oven to 350°F. Spray 11×7-inch baking dish with nonstick cooking spray.

4. Cut cold polenta into 12 (3½-inch) squares; arrange 6 squares in bottom of prepared dish. Spread with half of bell pepper mixture, half of vegetable mixture and 2 tablespoons Parmesan. Place remaining 6 squares polenta over Parmesan; top with remaining bell pepper and vegetable mixtures and Parmesan. Bake 20 minutes or until cheese is melted and polenta is golden brown. Cut into 6 wedges before serving.   *Makes 6 servings*

barley and wild rice pilaf

½ cup uncooked wild rice

2 tablespoons olive oil, divided

1 medium onion, chopped

1 cup uncooked pearl barley

3 cloves garlic, minced

4 cups chicken broth

1 large red bell pepper, cut into ¼-inch pieces

3 ounces fresh mushrooms, thinly sliced (about 1½ cups)

½ cup frozen green peas, thawed

½ cup shredded carrot

1 teaspoon dried oregano *or* 1 tablespoon chopped fresh oregano

1. Rinse rice in strainer under cold running water. Drain; set aside.

2. Heat 1 tablespoon oil in large saucepan over medium heat. Add onion; cook and stir about 10 minutes or until tender. Add barley, rice and garlic; cook and stir over medium heat 1 minute.

3. Stir in chicken broth. Bring to a boil over medium-high heat. Reduce heat to low; simmer, covered, about 1 hour or until barley and rice are tender.

4. Heat remaining 1 tablespoon oil in large skillet over medium-high heat. Add bell pepper, mushrooms, peas, carrot and oregano; cook and stir 5 to 6 minutes or until vegetables are tender.

5. Stir bell pepper mixture into rice mixture.   *Makes 8 servings*

pumpernickel bread (gluten-free)

1½ cups water

3 eggs

3 tablespoons vegetable oil

3 tablespoons molasses

1 teaspoon vinegar

2 cups brown rice flour

½ cup tapioca flour

½ cup potato starch flour

½ cup dry milk powder

3 tablespoons sugar

1 tablespoon xanthan gum*

1 tablespoon caraway seeds

1 tablespoon cocoa

2¼ teaspoons (1 packet) RED STAR® Active Dry Yeast *or* 1½ teaspoons
    QUICK•RISE™ Yeast or Bread Machine Yeast

1½ teaspoons salt

1 teaspoon grated orange peel

Xanthan gum can be found in health food stores.

Bread Machine Method

Have all ingredients at room temperature. Combine water, eggs, oil, molasses and vinegar; pour into baking pan.

Combine flours, milk powder, sugar, xanthan gum, caraway seeds, cocoa, yeast, salt and orange peel. Blend thoroughly in bowl with wire whisk or shake together in large resealing plastic food storage bag.*

Select white or basic cycle; start machine.

For bread machines with bake only cycle, select dough cycle for mixing and rising. Press stop when cycle is complete; then select the bake only cycle to complete bread.

After mixing action begins, help any unmixed ingredients into dough with rubber spatula, keeping to edges of batter to prevent interference with kneading blade.

When bake cycle is complete, remove pan from machine. Allow bread to remain in pan about 10 minutes, then invert pan and shake gently to remove bread. Cool upright on rack before slicing.

Mixer Method

In mixing bowl, combine water, eggs, oil, molasses and vinegar; mix well.

Combine flours, milk powder, sugar, xanthan gum, caraway seeds, cocoa, yeast, salt and orange peel. Blend thoroughly in bowl with wire whisk or shake together in large resealing plastic food storage bag.*

With mixer on low speed, gradually add flour mixture to mixing bowl until well blended. Beat about 10 minutes.

Pour batter into three 5×2½-inch greased bread pans; allow to rise about 1 hour. Bake at 375°F for 45 to 60 minutes or until toothpick comes out clean when inserted in center.

When baking is complete, remove pan from oven; let bread cool 10 minutes in pans. Remove from pans and cool completely on wire rack before slicing.

Makes 3 loaves

Gluten-free flours are very fine and need to be well blended before liquid is added to them.

pineapple wild rice

1 cup uncooked brown rice
½ cup uncooked wild rice
¼ cup margarine
2 cups sliced fresh mushrooms
1 cup chopped onion
1 cup finely chopped fresh DOLE® Tropical Gold® Pineapple
1 cup finely chopped dried apricots
½ cup toasted pine nuts
1 teaspoon chopped fresh thyme *or* ¼ teaspoon dried thyme leaves

• Cook brown rice and wild rice according to package directions, omitting oils.

• Melt margarine in large skillet. Stir in mushrooms and onion, cooking 10 minutes or until onion is tender.

• Stir pineapple, apricots, pine nuts and thyme into skillet. Stir in rices. Heat through. Serve hot or at room temperature. Garnish with fresh thyme sprig, if desired. Serve with lamb and green beans. *Makes 10 servings*

Prep Time: 75 minutes

brown rice with porcini mushrooms

2½ cups water
1 cup uncooked brown rice
½ cup dried porcini mushrooms
6 sun-dried tomato halves, cut into pieces
1 tablespoon dried minced onion
1 tablespoon butter
1 tablespoon snipped chives
1 tablespoon beef or vegetable bouillon granules
½ teaspoon dried minced garlic
¼ teaspoon dried thyme leaves
¼ teaspoon black pepper
¼ cup grated Parmesan cheese

1. Combine water, rice, mushrooms, sun-dried tomatoes, onion, butter, chives, bouillon, garlic, thyme and pepper in large saucepan. Stir to mix well; bring to a boil. Cover; reduce heat to medium and simmer 55 to 60 minutes or until rice is tender.

2. Stir in Parmesan cheese.

Makes 4 servings

brown rice with porcini mushrooms

south american chicken and quinoa

Tomato-Apricot Chutney (page 182)
1 teaspoon ground turmeric
1 teaspoon dried thyme
¾ teaspoon salt, divided
1 pound boneless skinless chicken breasts, cut into 1-inch pieces
2 tablespoons olive oil, divided
1 large green bell pepper, seeded and chopped
1 medium onion, chopped
1 cup uncooked quinoa
1 cup chicken broth
1 cup unsweetened coconut milk
1 teaspoon curry powder
¼ teaspoon ground ginger

1. Prepare Tomato-Apricot Chutney; set aside.

2. Combine turmeric, thyme and ¼ teaspoon salt in shallow dish. Dip 1 chicken piece at a time into spice mixture, coating all sides; set aside.

3. Heat 1 tablespoon oil in large heavy skillet over medium-high heat. Add bell pepper and onion. Cook and stir 2 minutes or until vegetables are crisp-tender. Remove from skillet with slotted spoon; set aside.

4. Add remaining 1 tablespoon oil to skillet. Add chicken pieces. Cook and stir 5 minutes or until chicken is cooked through.

5. Rinse quinoa in small strainer under cold water; drain well. Combine quinoa, chicken broth, coconut milk, curry, remaining ½ teaspoon salt and ginger in large heavy saucepan. Bring to a boil over high heat. Reduce heat to low; simmer, covered, 10 minutes.

6. Stir in chicken and pepper mixture; cook 5 minutes or until liquid is absorbed. Serve with Tomato-Apricot Chutney. *Makes 4 servings*

continued on page 182

south american chicken and quinoa, continued

tomato-apricot chutney

¾ cup apple cider or apple juice
¾ cup finely diced dried apricots
½ cup currants or golden raisins
3 to 4 tablespoons cider vinegar
1 can (14½ ounces) diced tomatoes, drained
1 tablespoon dark brown sugar
1 teaspoon ground ginger
⅛ teaspoon ground cloves

1. Combine apple cider, apricots, currants and vinegar in small saucepan. Bring to a boil over high heat. Reduce heat to low; simmer, covered, 10 minutes.

2. Stir in tomatoes, brown sugar, ginger and cloves. Simmer, uncovered, about 5 minutes or until liquid is absorbed.

cornmeal butter cookies

1 cup (2 sticks) unsalted butter, softened
⅓ cup plus 2 tablespoons sugar, divided
1 egg
¼ cup pure maple syrup
½ teaspoon salt
2 cups corn flour
½ cup cornmeal (not coarse-ground)

1. Preheat oven to 350°F. Line 2 cookie sheets with parchment paper.

2. Beat butter and ⅓ cup sugar in medium bowl with electric mixer at medium-high speed. Beat in egg, maple syrup and salt until combined. Add corn flour and cornmeal gradually, mixing well. Refrigerate dough 30 minutes.

3. Shape dough into 1-inch balls. Place 1 inch apart on prepared cookie sheets. Flatten dough to ⅓-inch thickness using the bottom of a glass dipped in remaining 2 tablespoons sugar.

4. Bake 12 to 14 minutes or until edges are golden brown. Cool 2 minutes on cookie sheets. Remove to wire rack to cool completely.   *Makes 4 dozen cookies*

brown rice and vegetable stuffed squash

　2 large acorn or golden acorn squash (about 1½ pounds each)
　1 cup uncooked brown rice
　2 cups broccoli florets, chopped
　½ teaspoon salt
　½ teaspoon black pepper
　¼ cup chopped almonds, toasted
　¾ cup shredded sharp Cheddar or smoked Gouda cheese

1. Cut squash in half crosswise; scrape out and discard seeds. Trim off stems and pointed ends to allow squash to stand when filled. Place squash halves cut sides down on microwavable plate; microwave on HIGH 12 to 15 minutes, or until almost tender when pierced. Place squash halves in 13×9-inch baking pan, cut sides up. Cover; let stand until ready to fill. Preheat oven to 375°F.

2. Meanwhile, cook rice according to package directions adding broccoli, salt and pepper during last 5 minutes of cooking. Stir in almonds.

3. Mound rice mixture into squash, overflowing into dish if necessary; sprinkle with cheese. Bake 20 to 25 minutes or until squash is tender and cheese is melted.

Makes 4 servings

fruited rice

2¼ cups water
½ cup uncooked wild rice
½ cup uncooked brown rice
2 tablespoons dried minced onion
1 tablespoon dried parsley flakes
1 tablespoon butter
2 teaspoons chicken bouillon granules
2 teaspoons firmly packed brown sugar
½ teaspoon dried thyme
¼ teaspoon black pepper
⅛ teaspoon ground red pepper
¼ to ½ cup orange juice
¼ cup chopped dried apricots
¼ cup chopped dried cranberries or cherries
¼ cup raisins or currants

1. Combine water, wild rice, brown rice, parsley, butter, bouillon, sugar, thyme, black pepper and red pepper in large saucepan. Bring to a boil over high heat. Cover; reduce heat and simmer 45 to 50 minutes or until rice is almost tender.

2. Stir in orange juice, apricots, cranberries and raisins. Simmer, uncovered, 15 minutes or until rice is tender. *Makes 4 servings*

grain
of advice

Wild rice isn't really rice at all. It's a long-grain marsh grass native to the Midwestern United States. The nutritional profile of wild rice is similar to other whole grains and includes a healthy helping of B vitamins, fiber and protein. In the past, wild rice was considered a luxury item since it had to be discovered and then harvested by hand. Today wild rice is commercially cultivated and much more affordable.

fruited rice

honey nut dressing

1 bag SUCCESS® Brown Rice
1 tablespoon reduced-calorie margarine
¼ cup chopped walnuts
¾ cup chopped onion
¾ cup chopped celery
½ cup raisins
2 tablespoons chopped fresh parsley (optional)
2 tablespoons honey
1 tablespoon lemon juice
¼ teaspoon salt
¼ teaspoon pepper

Prepare rice according to package directions.

Melt margarine in large skillet over medium heat. Add walnuts; cook and stir until lightly toasted. Add onion and celery; cook and stir until crisp-tender. Stir in rice and remaining ingredients. Heat thoroughly, stirring occasionally.

Makes 6 servings

Dressing (or do you call it stuffing?) makes an excellent side dish even if it's not Thanksgiving. Don't limit it to bread cubes. Brown rice, barley and other whole grains make nutritious substitutes. These grains do more than absorb the flavor of seasonings. They bring a nutty savor of their own. Try serving a whole grain dressing with roasted or grilled meat, poultry or fish. You'll be adding nutrition as well as a tasty side dish.

honey nut dressing

smart snacking

The USDA recommends that we get at least three servings of whole grains every day. Why not take a break with a cracker, snack mix or bar made with whole grains? There are plenty of delicious choices. If crunch is your thing, try Snackin' Cinnamon Popcorn. If you hunger for a taste of something sweet, Honey Carrot Snacking Cake should fill the bill. Now it's easy to satisfy snack cravings without the guilt.

whole wheat pizza with asparagus and feta

  1 cup warm (110°F) water
  1 tablespoon active dry yeast
1¼ cups whole wheat flour
 ¼ cup soy flour*
  1 teaspoon sea salt
  2 tablespoons olive oil
  2 teaspoons fresh rosemary
  5 to 10 cooked asparagus spears, cut into bite-size pieces
 12 to 15 grape tomatoes, cut into halves
 ½ cup crumbled feta cheese

Soy flour can be purchased at natural food stores.

1. Combine water and yeast in medium bowl; let stand until foamy. Add flours and mix until well combined. Stir in salt. Cover and let rise in warm place 45 minutes.

2. Preheat oven to 400°F. Lightly spray 12-inch pizza pan with nonstick cooking spray. Scrape dough out of bowl and onto prepared pan. Press dough to edge of pan with floured hands. Bake 15 minutes or until edges are brown and crisp.

3. Brush with olive oil and sprinkle with rosemary. Top with asparagus, tomatoes and feta. Bake 5 minutes until toppings are heated through.

Makes 8 servings

rosemary wine crackers

1 cup whole wheat flour
1 tablespoon chopped fresh rosemary
⅛ teaspoon salt
3 tablespoons olive oil
4 to 6 tablespoons wine (preferably a fruity white or rosé)
Coarse salt (optional)

1. Preheat oven to 400°F. Line cookie sheet with parchment paper; dust lightly with flour. Place flour, rosemary and salt in food processor. Pulse 30 seconds to combine.

2. With motor running, add oil and wine gradually through feedtube. When mixture becomes dough ball on top of blade, stop adding wine.

3. Transfer dough to prepared cookie sheet. Roll dough as thin as possible (⅛-inch or less) on cookie sheet. Sprinkle with coarse salt, if desired, and roll lightly to make salt adhere. Score crackers with knife or pizza cutter into squares or diamonds.

4. Bake 10 to 15 minutes or until crackers begin to brown around edges, rotating pan halfway through baking time. Remove to wire rack to cool. Break into individual crackers. Store in airtight container. To re-crisp, place in 350°F oven for 5 minutes.

Makes about 2 dozen crackers

Making crackers is surprisingly easy. This recipe can be easily doubled or adjusted to suit personal tastes. Because crackers don't need to rise, whole wheat flour works unusually well. You could also swap out some of the wheat flour for rye or even buckwheat flour. Instead of wine, you could use fruit juice or even water. Perhaps the best part of making your own crackers is that you decide what ingredients go into them.

rosemary wine crackers

banana roll-ups

¼ cup smooth or crunchy almond butter

2 tablespoons mini chocolate chips

1 to 2 tablespoons milk

1 (8-inch) whole wheat flour tortilla

1 large banana, peeled

1. Combine almond butter, chocolate chips and 1 tablespoon milk in medium microwavable bowl. Microwave on MEDIUM (50%) 40 seconds. Stir well and repeat if necessary to melt chocolate. Add more milk if necessary for desired consistency.

2. Spread almond butter mixture on tortilla. Place banana on one side of tortilla and roll up tightly. Cut into 8 slices. *Makes 4 servings*

baked caramel corn

Nonstick cooking spray

6 quarts popped JOLLY TIME® Pop Corn

1 cup butter or margarine

2 cups firmly packed brown sugar

½ cup light or dark corn syrup

1 teaspoon salt

1 teaspoon vanilla

½ teaspoon baking soda

Preheat oven to 250°F. Coat bottom and sides of large roasting pan with nonstick cooking spray. Place popped popcorn in roasting pan. In heavy saucepan, slowly melt butter; stir in brown sugar, corn syrup and salt. Bring to a boil, stirring constantly; boil without stirring 5 minutes. Remove from heat; stir in vanilla and baking soda. Gradually pour over popped popcorn, mixing well. Bake 1 hour, stirring every 15 minutes. Remove from oven; cool completely. Break apart and store in tightly covered container. *Makes about 6 quarts*

honey carrot snacking cake

½ cup butter or margarine, softened
1 cup honey
2 eggs
2 cups finely grated carrots
½ cup golden raisins
⅓ cup chopped nuts (optional)
¼ cup orange juice
2 teaspoons vanilla
1 cup all-purpose flour
1 cup whole wheat flour
2 teaspoons baking powder
1½ teaspoons ground cinnamon
1 teaspoon baking soda
½ teaspoon salt
½ teaspoon ground ginger
¼ teaspoon ground nutmeg

Cream butter in large bowl. Gradually beat in honey until light and fluffy. Add eggs, one at a time, beating well after each addition. Combine carrots, raisins, nuts, if desired, orange juice and vanilla in medium bowl. Combine dry ingredients in separate large bowl. Add dry ingredients to creamed mixture alternately with carrot mixture, beginning and ending with dry ingredients. Pour batter into greased 13×9×2-inch pan. Bake at 350°F 35 to 45 minutes or until wooden pick inserted near center comes out clean. *Makes 12 servings*

Favorite recipe from **National Honey Board**

honey fig whole wheat muffins

1 cup whole wheat flour
½ cup all-purpose flour
½ cup wheat germ
2 teaspoons baking powder
1 teaspoon ground cinnamon
½ teaspoon salt
½ teaspoon ground nutmeg
½ cup milk
½ cup honey
¼ cup (½ stick) butter, melted
1 egg
1 cup chopped dried figs
½ cup chopped walnuts

1. Preheat oven to 375°F. Grease 12 standard (2½-inch) muffin cups or line with paper baking cups.

2. Combine flours, wheat germ, baking powder, cinnamon, salt and nutmeg in large bowl. Blend milk, honey, butter and egg in small bowl. Stir into flour mixture just until moistened. Fold in figs and walnuts. Spoon evenly into prepared muffin cups.

3. Bake 20 minutes or until edges are lightly browned and toothpick inserted into centers comes out clean. Remove from pan. *Makes 12 muffins*

honey fig whole wheat muffins

pb berry bars

½ cup reduced-fat peanut butter

½ cup semisweet mini chocolate chips, divided

¼ cup packed brown sugar

¼ cup canola oil, divided

1 teaspoon ground cinnamon

2 cups quick oats

¾ cup finely chopped strawberries

1. Mix peanut butter, 5 tablespoons chocolate chips, 2½ tablespoons oil, sugar and cinnamon in skillet. Cook and stir over low heat until melted. Remove from heat; add oats and stir until well blended. Press mixture firmly into into 9-inch square baking pan with spatula to make crust. Allow to cool; sprinkle strawberries over top.

2. Place remaining chocolate chips and oil in small saucepan. Cook and stir over low heat until melted; drizzle over strawberries. Cover with foil and freeze at least 2 hours.

3. To serve, let stand 10 minutes at room temperature before cutting into squares. Store leftovers in freezer. *Makes 16 servings*

whole grain cereal bars

5 to 6 cups assorted whole grain ready-to-eat cereals
1 bag (10 ounces) large marshmallows
¼ cup (½ stick) butter
¼ cup old-fashioned oats

1. Butter 13×9-inch baking pan. Place large chunks of cereal in resealable food storage bag and lightly crush with rolling pin.

2. Place marshmallows and butter in large saucepan or Dutch oven. Melt over medium-low heat, stirring until smooth. Remove pan from heat.

3. Add cereal to marshmallow mixture; stir to combine. Pat cereal mixture evenly into prepared pan using buttered hands or waxed paper to prevent sticking. Sprinkle with oats. Let cool at room temperature until firm. Cut into bars to serve.

Makes about 24 bars

s'more gorp

2 cups honey graham cereal
2 cups low-fat granola cereal
2 cups multi-grain cereal squares
2 tablespoons butter
1 tablespoon honey
¼ teaspoon ground cinnamon
¾ cup miniature marshmallows
½ cup dried fruit bits or raisins
¼ cup mini semisweet chocolate chips

1. Preheat oven to 275°F.

2. Combine cereals in nonstick 15×10×1-inch jelly-roll pan. Melt butter in small saucepan; stir in honey and cinnamon. Pour butter mixture evenly over cereal mixture; toss until cereal is well coated. Spread mixture evenly in bottom of pan. Bake 35 to 40 minutes or until crisp, stirring after 20 minutes. Cool completely.

3. Add marshmallows, fruit bits and chocolate chips; toss to mix.

Makes 16 servings

sunflower and oat granola bars

1½ cups rolled oats

¾ cup sunflower kernels (raw or roasted)

½ cup coconut

¼ cup wheat germ

¼ cup whole wheat flour

¼ teaspoon ground cinnamon

⅛ teaspoon ground nutmeg

½ cup sunflower margarine or butter

½ cup packed brown sugar

⅓ cup honey

In medium bowl, stir together oats, sunflower kernels, coconut, wheat germ, flour, cinnamon and nutmeg. Set aside. In saucepan or microwave, melt margarine. Stir brown sugar and honey into melted margarine; bring to a boil. Remove from heat. Pour margarine mixture over oats mixture; stir until well coated. Press mixture into greased 8×8×2-inch baking pan. Sprinkle with additional sunflower kernels and coconut, if desired. Bake in 350°F oven 35 to 45 minutes or until slightly browned around edges. Remove from oven. While bars are still warm, press surface gently with back of spoon to flatten and score into bars with knife. Cool completely before cutting into bars. *Makes 12 bars*

Favorite recipe from **National Sunflower Association**

There are many products claiming whole grain goodness these days. It pays to look beyond the advertising hype. If the label doesn't say 100% whole grain, it probably isn't. Multigrain or natural grain breads or cereals may be delicious and nutritious but they are not necessarily made of whole grains. Check the ingredients list for words like whole wheat flour (not just wheat flour) or whole grain oats to be sure.

cinnamon trail mix

    2 cups corn cereal squares
    2 cups whole wheat cereal squares
 1½ cups oyster crackers
    ½ cup broken sesame snack sticks
    2 tablespoons butter, melted
    1 teaspoon ground cinnamon
    ¼ teaspoon ground nutmeg
    ½ cup fruit-flavored candy pieces

1. Preheat oven to 350°F. Spray 13×9-inch baking pan with nonstick cooking spray.

2. Place cereals, oyster crackers and sesame sticks in prepared pan; mix lightly.

3. Combine butter, cinnamon and nutmeg in small bowl; mix well. Drizzle evenly over cereal mixture; toss to coat.

4. Bake 12 to 14 minutes or until golden brown, stirring gently after 6 minutes. Cool completely. Stir in candies.   *Makes 8 (¾-cup) servings*

peanut butter-apple wraps

    ¾ cup creamy peanut butter
    4 (7-inch) whole wheat tortillas
    ¾ cup finely chopped apple
    ⅓ cup shredded carrot
    ⅓ cup low-fat granola without raisins
    1 tablespoon toasted wheat germ

Spread peanut butter on one side of each tortilla. Sprinkle each tortilla evenly with apple, carrot, granola and wheat germ. Roll up tightly; cut in half. Serve immediately or refrigerate until ready to serve.   *Makes 4 servings*

Prep Time: 5 minutes
Chill Time: 2 hours

cinnamon trail mix

tuna schooners

2 (3-ounce) cans water-packed light tuna, drained
½ cup finely chopped apple
¼ cup shredded carrot
⅓ cup reduced-fat ranch salad dressing
2 whole wheat English muffins, split and lightly toasted
8 tortilla chips

1. Combine tuna, apple and carrot in medium bowl. Add salad dressing; stir to combine.

2. Spread one fourth of tuna mixture on each muffin half. Press chips firmly into tuna mixture on each muffin half.   *Makes 4 servings*

cinnamon-raisin roll-ups

4 ounces reduced-fat cream cheese, softened
½ cup shredded carrot
¼ cup raisins
1 tablespoon honey
¼ teaspoon ground cinnamon
4 (7- to 8-inch) whole wheat flour tortillas
8 thin apple wedges

1. Combine cream cheese, carrot, raisins, honey and cinnamon in small bowl.

2. Spread mixture evenly on tortillas, leaving ½-inch border around edge of each tortilla. Place 2 apple wedges down center of each tortilla; roll up. Wrap in plastic wrap. Refrigerate until ready to serve.   *Makes 4 servings*

mixed grain tabbouleh

1 cup uncooked brown rice
3 cups vegetable broth, divided
½ cup uncooked bulgur wheat
1 cup chopped tomatoes
½ cup minced green onions
¼ cup fresh mint leaves, chopped
¼ cup fresh basil leaves, chopped
¼ cup fresh oregano sprigs, chopped
3 tablespoons fresh lemon juice
3 tablespoons olive oil
½ teaspoon salt
½ teaspoon black pepper

1. Combine brown rice and 2 cups chicken broth in medium saucepan. Bring to a boil over medium-high heat. Reduce heat to low. Simmer, covered, 45 minutes or until broth is absorbed and rice is tender; cool.

2. Meanwhile combine bulgur and remaining 1 cup chicken broth in small saucepan. Bring to a boil over medium-high heat. Reduce heat to low. Simmer, covered, 15 minutes or until broth is absorbed and bulgur is fluffy.

3. Combine tomatoes, green onions, chopped herbs, lemon juice, oil, salt and pepper in large bowl. Stir in bulgur and rice. Cool to room temperature.

Makes 6 servings

wheat germ wafers

1 cup all-purpose flour
1 cup whole wheat flour
1 cup wheat germ
¼ cup sugar
1½ teaspoons salt
1 teaspoon baking powder
¾ cup water
⅓ cup butter, melted
Garlic salt or salt

1. Preheat oven to 350°F. Combine flours, wheat germ, sugar, salt and baking powder in large bowl.

2. Combine water and butter in small bowl. Add water mixture to flour mixture; stir until mixture forms soft dough that forms a ball.

3. Turn out dough onto well-floured surface. Knead dough gently 10 to 12 times. Divide dough in thirds. Roll out one piece of dough into 12×10-inch rectangle with lightly floured rolling pin. (Keep remaining dough covered with towel.)

4. Place rolling pin on one side of dough. Gently roll dough over rolling pin once. Carefully lift rolling pin and dough, unrolling dough over ungreased cookie sheet.

5. Cut dough into 30 (2-inch) squares with pastry wheel or floured knife. Sprinkle with garlic salt. Repeat with remaining dough.

6. Bake 15 to 20 minutes or until wafers are lightly browned. Immediately remove from cookie sheets; cool on wire racks. Store in airtight container up to 3 days.

Makes 7½ dozen crackers

perfect pita pizzas

    2 rounds whole wheat pita bread
 ½ cup pasta or pizza sauce
 ¾ cup (3 ounces) shredded mozzarella cheese
    1 small zucchini, sliced ¼ inch thick
 ½ small carrot, peeled and sliced
    2 cherry tomatoes, halved
 ¼ small green bell pepper, sliced

1. Preheat oven to 375°F. Line baking sheet with foil; set aside.

2. Using small scissors, carefully split each pita around edge; separate to form 2 rounds.

3. Place rounds, rough sides up, on prepared baking sheet. Bake 5 minutes.

4. Spread 2 tablespoons pasta sauce onto each round; sprinkle with cheese. Top with vegetables to create faces. Bake 10 to 12 minutes or until cheese melts.

Makes 4 servings

Let the kids (or playful grown-ups) decorate their own pita pizzas. Whole wheat pita bread can also be easily turned into a crunchy, healthy chip. Just separate it around the edge as for this recipe, then tear each round into chip-sized pieces and bake at 350°F for 15 minutes or until browned and crisp.

spice-prune loaf

1 cup chopped pitted prunes
½ cup prune juice
1 cup all-purpose flour
1 cup whole wheat flour
1 teaspoon baking powder
¾ teaspoon ground cinnamon
½ teaspoon baking soda
¼ teaspoon ground ginger
⅛ teaspoon salt
2 egg whites
⅓ cup molasses
3 tablespoons canola oil
¼ teaspoon vanilla

1. Preheat oven to 350°F. Spray 8×4-inch loaf pan with nonstick cooking spray. Combine prunes and prune juice in small saucepan. Bring to a boil over medium-high heat. Remove from heat; let stand 5 minutes.

2. Combine flours, baking powder, cinnamon, baking soda, ginger and salt in medium bowl. Combine egg whites, molasses, oil and vanilla in small bowl. Add to flour mixture and stir until just blended. Add prune mixture; stir until just blended.

3. Pour batter into prepared pan. Bake 55 to 60 minutes or until toothpick inserted into center comes out clean. Cool in pan on wire rack 10 minutes. Remove bread from pan; cool completely on wire rack. Wrap and store overnight at room temperature before slicing.   *Makes 16 servings*

savory pita chips

2 rounds whole wheat pita bread
Olive oil cooking spray
3 tablespoons grated Parmesan cheese
1 teaspoon dried basil
¼ teaspoon garlic powder

1. Preheat oven to 350°F. Line baking sheet with foil; set aside.

2. Using scissors, carefully cut each pita bread around edges to form 2 rounds. Cut each round into 6 wedges.

3. Place wedges, rough side down, on prepared baking sheet; coat lightly with cooking spray. Turn wedges over; spray again.

4. Combine Parmesan cheese, basil and garlic powder in small bowl; sprinkle evenly over pita wedges.

5. Bake 12 to 14 minutes or until golden brown. Cool completely.

Makes 4 servings

Cinnamon Crisps: Substitute butter-flavored cooking spray for olive oil cooking spray, and 1 tablespoon sugar mixed with ¼ teaspoon ground cinnamon for Parmesan cheese, basil and garlic powder.

snackin' cinnamon popcorn

1 tablespoon brown sugar
1½ teaspoons salt
1½ teaspoons cinnamon
8 cups hot air-popped popcorn
Butter-flavored cooking spray

1. Combine brown sugar, salt and cinnamon in small bowl; mix well.

2. Spread hot popped popcorn onto jelly-roll pan. Coat popcorn with cooking spray; immediately sprinkle cinnamon mixture over top. Serve immediately or store in container at room temperature up to 2 days.
Makes 4 servings

savory pita chips

serious sweets

Get sweet on whole grains and you'll be amazed at how easy they are to add to luscious cookies, cakes and other treats. Once there's whole wheat flour in your pantry (or better yet, your refrigerator or freezer), you can use it in everything from Whole Wheat Brownies to Whole Wheat Chocolate Sheet Cake. You'll be adding a wholesome twist to your family's favorites and they probably won't even notice. Now that's a sweet deal.

oats and apple tart

1½ cups quick oats

½ cup brown sugar, divided

1 tablespoon plus ¼ teaspoon ground cinnamon, divided

5 tablespoons butter, melted

2 medium sweet apples, such as Golden Delicious, unpeeled, cored and thinly sliced

1 teaspoon lemon juice

¼ cup water

1 envelope unflavored gelatin

½ cup apple juice concentrate

1 package (8 ounces) reduced-fat cream cheese, softened

⅛ teaspoon ground nutmeg

1. Preheat oven to 350°F. Combine oats, ¼ cup brown sugar and 1 tablespoon cinnamon in medium bowl. Add butter and stir until combined. Press onto bottom and up side of 9-inch pie plate. Bake 7 minutes or until set. Cool on wire rack.

2. Toss apple slices with lemon juice in small bowl; set aside. Place water in small saucepan. Sprinkle gelatin over water; let stand 3 to 5 minutes. Stir in apple juice concentrate. Cook and stir over medium heat until gelatin is dissolved. *Do not boil.* Remove from heat and set aside.

3. Beat cream cheese in medium bowl with electric mixer until fluffy and smooth. Add remaining ¼ cup brown sugar, ¼ teaspoon cinnamon and nutmeg. Mix until smooth. Slowly beat in gelatin mixture on low speed until blended and creamy, about 1 minute. *Do not overbeat.*

4. Arrange apple slices in crust. Pour cream cheese mixture evenly over top. Refrigerate 2 hours or until set. Garnish as desired.   *Makes 8 servings*

basic oatmeal cookies

2 cups old-fashioned oats
1⅓ cups all-purpose flour
¾ teaspoon baking soda
½ teaspoon baking powder
½ teaspoon salt
1 cup packed light brown sugar
¾ cup (1½ sticks) butter, softened
¼ cup granulated sugar
1 egg
1 tablespoon honey
1 teaspoon vanilla

1. Preheat oven to 350°F. Line cookie sheets with parchment paper. Combine oats, flour, baking soda, baking powder and salt in medium bowl.

2. Combine brown sugar, butter and granulated sugar in large bowl; beat with electric mixer at medium speed until well blended. Beat on high speed until light and fluffy. Add egg, honey and vanilla; beat at medium speed until well blended. Gradually add flour mixture, about ½ cup at a time. Drop dough by tablespoonfuls 2 inches apart onto prepared cookie sheets.

3. Bake 11 to 15 minutes or until cookies are puffed and golden. *Do not overbake.* Cool 5 minutes on cookie sheets. Remove to wire racks; cool completely.

Makes 3 dozen cookies

northwoods buttermilk cake

2 cups all-purpose flour
1 cup whole wheat flour
2 teaspoons baking soda
1 teaspoon ground cinnamon
½ teaspoon salt
½ teaspoon ground nutmeg
½ cup reduced calorie margarine
1 cup packed brown sugar
1 teaspoon vanilla
5 egg whites
⅔ cup unsweetened applesauce
1 cup buttermilk
2 cups cooked wild rice
    Powdered sugar (optional)

Preheat oven to 350°F. Spray 13×9-inch pan with nonstick cooking spray; lightly flour. Combine flours, baking soda, cinnamon, salt and nutmeg in medium bowl. Beat margarine with electric mixer on medium speed for 30 seconds in large mixing bowl. Add brown sugar and vanilla; beat until fluffy. Add egg whites; beat well. Add applesauce, blending well. Add dry ingredients and buttermilk alternately to mixture, blending well. Stir in wild rice. Pour into prepared pan. Bake 45 to 50 minutes or until wooden pick inserted in center comes out clean. Do not overbake. Cool. Sprinkle with powdered sugar, if desired.   *Makes 16 servings*

Favorite recipe from **Minnesota Cultivated Wild Rice Council**

deep dark chocolate drops

¾ cup all-purpose flour

½ cup whole wheat flour

¼ cup unsweetened cocoa powder

½ teaspoon salt

½ teaspoon baking soda

1½ cups semisweet chocolate chips, divided

½ cup (1 stick) butter, softened

½ cup granulated sugar

¼ cup packed light brown sugar

1 egg, lightly beaten

2 tablespoons milk

1 teaspoon vanilla

1. Preheat oven to 350°F. Lightly grease cookie sheets. Combine flours, cocoa, salt and baking soda in medium bowl.

2. Place ½ cup chocolate chips in small microwavable bowl. Microwave on HIGH 1 minute; stir. Microwave at additional 30-second intervals until chips are melted and smooth. Let cool slightly.

3. Beat butter, granulated sugar and brown sugar in large bowl with electric mixer until light and fluffy. Add egg, milk, vanilla and melted chocolate; beat until well blended. Add flour mixture; beat just until blended. Stir in remaining 1 cup chocolate chips. Drop dough by tablespoonfuls 2 inches apart onto prepared cookie sheets.

4. Bake 10 to 11 minutes or until set and no longer shiny. Cool 2 minutes on cookie sheets. Remove to wire racks; cool completely. *Makes about 3 dozen cookies*

peach oatmeal cookies

¾ cup granulated sugar

¾ cup packed brown sugar

⅔ cup margarine

2 eggs

1½ teaspoons vanilla

1½ cups whole wheat flour

2 teaspoons baking powder

1 teaspoon salt

2½ cups rolled oats

1½ cups diced peeled fresh California peaches

1 cup raisins

1. Preheat oven to 350°F.

2. Beat sugars, margarine, eggs and vanilla in large mixing bowl with electric mixer at medium speed.

3. Combine flour, baking powder and salt in separate bowl. Add to egg mixture and beat at low speed 2 to 3 minutes or until smooth.

4. Stir in oats, peaches and raisins. Drop by tablespoonfuls onto nonstick baking sheet.

5. Bake 10 to 15 minutes or until golden. *Makes 3 dozen cookies*

Favorite recipe from **California Tree Fruit Agreement**

chocolate-hazelnut rounds

¾ cup all-purpose flour
½ cup whole wheat flour
½ teaspoon salt
½ teaspoon baking soda
½ cup (1 stick) butter, softened
½ cup chocolate-hazelnut spread*
½ cup granulated sugar
¼ cup packed light brown sugar
1 egg, lightly beaten
1 teaspoon vanilla
1 cup white chocolate chips
1 teaspoon shortening

Can be found in most supermarkets near the peanut butter.

1. Preheat oven to 350°F. Lightly grease cookie sheets. Combine flours, salt and baking soda in medium bowl.

2. Beat butter, chocolate-hazelnut spread and sugars in large bowl until light and fluffy. Add egg and vanilla; beat until well blended. Add flour mixture; beat just until blended. Shape dough by level teaspoons into balls; place 2 inches apart on prepared cookie sheets.

3. Bake 10 to 12 minutes or until edges are lightly browned. Cool 1 minute on cookie sheets. Remove to wire racks; cool completely.

4. Place white chocolate chips and shortening in small microwavable bowl. Microwave on HIGH 1 minute; stir. Microwave at additional 30-second intervals until chips are melted and mixture is smooth. Dip cookies into white chocolate mixture; let stand until set. *Makes about 6 dozen cookies*

blueberry crisp

3 cups cooked brown rice

3 cups fresh blueberries*

¼ cup plus 3 tablespoons firmly packed brown sugar, divided

Vegetable cooking spray

⅓ cup rice bran

¼ cup whole-wheat flour

¼ cup chopped walnuts

1 teaspoon ground cinnamon

3 tablespoons margarine

Or substitute frozen unsweetened blueberries for the fresh blueberries, if desired. Thaw and drain before using. Or, substitute your choice of fresh fruit or combinations of fruit for the blueberries, if desired.

Combine rice, blueberries and 3 tablespoons sugar. Coat 8 individual custard cups or 2-quart baking dish with cooking spray. Place rice mixture in cups or baking dish; set aside. Combine bran, flour, walnuts, remaining ¼ cup sugar and cinnamon in bowl. Cut in margarine with pastry blender until mixture resembles coarse meal. Sprinkle over rice mixture. Bake at 375°F. for 15 to 20 minutes or until thoroughly heated. Serve warm. *Makes 8 servings*

Microwave Directions: Prepare as directed, using 2-quart microproof baking dish. Cook, uncovered, on HIGH 4 to 5 minutes, rotating dish once during cooking time. Let stand 5 minutes. Serve warm.

*Favorite recipe from **USA Rice***

Blueberries and whole grains are a delicious and nutritious combination. Blueberries are bursting with flavor and loaded with antioxidants. Purchase berries that are firm and deep blue. Don't wash them until you're ready to use them. Blueberries also freeze very well, so stock up when they're in season.

cocoa crackles

¾ cup all-purpose flour

½ cup whole wheat flour

⅓ cup unsweetened cocoa powder

½ teaspoon salt

½ teaspoon baking soda

½ cup (1 stick) butter, softened

½ cup granulated sugar

¼ cup packed light brown sugar

2 eggs, lightly beaten

1 teaspoon vanilla

Powdered sugar

1. Preheat oven to 350°F. Lightly grease cookie sheets. Combine flours, cocoa, salt and baking soda in medium bowl.

2. Beat butter, granulated sugar and brown sugar in large bowl with electric mixer until light and fluffy. Add eggs and vanilla; beat until well blended. Add flour mixture; beat just until blended.

3. Place powdered sugar in shallow bowl. Shape dough by heaping teaspoons into balls. Roll balls in powdered sugar; place 2 inches apart on prepared cookie sheets.

4. Bake about 11 minutes or until set and no longer shiny. Cool 2 minutes on cookie sheets. Remove to wire racks; cool completely.   *Makes about 3½ dozen cookies*

whole grain chippers

1 cup (2 sticks) butter, softened
1 cup packed light brown sugar
⅔ cup granulated sugar
2 eggs
1 teaspoon baking soda
1 teaspoon vanilla
  Pinch salt
2 cups old-fashioned oats
1 cup all-purpose flour
1 cup whole wheat flour
1 package (12 ounces) semisweet chocolate chips
1 cup sunflower seeds

1. Preheat oven to 375°F. Lightly grease cookie sheets or line with parchment paper.

2. Beat butter, sugars and eggs in large bowl with electric mixer until fluffy. Beat in baking soda, vanilla and salt. Blend in oats and flours to make stiff dough. Stir in chocolate chips. Shape rounded teaspoonfuls of dough into balls; roll in sunflower seeds. Place 2 inches apart on prepared cookie sheets.

3. Bake 8 to 10 minutes or until firm. Do not overbake. Cool 2 minutes on cookie sheets. Remove to wire racks; cool completely. *Makes about 6 dozen cookies*

baked banana doughnuts

2 ripe bananas, mashed
2 egg whites
1 tablespoon vegetable oil
1 cup packed brown sugar
1½ cups all-purpose flour
¾ cup whole wheat flour
2 teaspoons baking powder
½ teaspoon baking soda
¼ teaspoon pumpkin pie spice
1 tablespoon granulated sugar
2 tablespoons chopped walnuts (optional)

Preheat oven to 425°F. Spray baking sheet with nonstick cooking spray. Beat bananas, egg whites, oil and brown sugar in large bowl. Add flours, baking powder, baking soda and pumpkin pie spice. Mix until well blended. Let stand for five minutes for dough to rise. Scoop out heaping tablespoonfuls of dough onto prepared baking sheet. Using thin rubber spatula or butter knife round out doughnut hole in center of dough (if dough sticks to knife or spatula spray with cooking spray). With spatula, smooth outside edges of dough into round doughnut shape. Repeat until all dough is used. Sprinkle with granulated sugar and walnuts, if desired. Bake 6 to 10 minutes or until tops are golden.

Makes about 22 doughnuts

Variation: Use 8 ounces solid pack pumpkin instead of bananas to make pumpkin doughnuts.

*Favorite recipe from **The Sugar Association, Inc.***

whole wheat brownies

½ cup whole wheat flour

½ teaspoon baking soda

¼ teaspoon salt

½ cup (1 stick) butter

1 cup packed brown sugar

⅓ cup unsweetened cocoa powder

½ cup semisweet chocolate chips

1 teaspoon vanilla

2 eggs

1. Preheat oven to 350°F. Grease 8-inch square baking pan. Combine flour, baking soda and salt in small bowl.

2. Melt butter in large saucepan over low heat. Add brown sugar; cook and stir until sugar is completely dissolved and smooth about 4 minutes. Remove pan from heat and stir in cocoa until smooth. Add flour mixture and stir until smooth. Stir in vanilla and chocolate chips. Beat in eggs. Spoon batter into prepared pan.

3. Bake 15 to 20 minutes or until toothpick inserted into center comes out almost clean.

Makes 16 brownies

pumpkin oatmeal cookies

1 cup all-purpose flour
1 teaspoon ground cinnamon
½ teaspoon salt
½ teaspoon ground nutmeg
¼ teaspoon baking soda
1½ cups packed light brown sugar
½ cup (1 stick) butter, softened
1 egg
1 teaspoon vanilla
½ cup solid-pack pumpkin
2 cups old-fashioned oats
1 cup dried cranberries (optional)

1. Preheat oven to 350°F. Line cookie sheets with parchment paper. Sift flour, cinnamon, salt, nutmeg and baking soda into medium bowl.

2. Beat brown sugar and butter in large bowl with electric mixer at medium speed about 5 minutes or until light and fluffy. Beat in egg and vanilla. Add pumpkin; beat at low speed until blended. Beat in flour mixture just until blended. Add oats; mix well. Stir in cranberries, if desired. Drop batter by heaping tablespoonfuls about 2 inches apart onto prepared cookie sheets.

3. Bake 12 minutes or until golden brown. Cool on cookie sheets 1 minute. Remove to wire racks; cool completely. *Makes about 2 dozen cookies*

chunky double chocolate cookies

4 squares (1 ounce each) unsweetened chocolate
1 cup all-purpose flour
1 cup whole wheat flour
1½ teaspoons baking powder
½ teaspoon salt
1½ cups packed brown sugar
¾ cup (1½ sticks) butter, softened
1 teaspoon vanilla
2 eggs
12 ounces white chocolate, chopped *or* 1 package (12 ounces) white chocolate chips
1 cup chopped nuts (optional)

1. Preheat oven to 350°F. Melt unsweetened chocolate according to package directions; cool slightly.

2. Combine flours, baking powder and salt in medium bowl. Beat brown sugar, butter and vanilla in large bowl with electric mixer at medium speed until light and fluffy. Add eggs; beat until well blended. Beat in melted chocolate. Gradually add flour mixture, mixing well after each addition. Stir in white chocolate and nuts. Drop by heaping tablespoonfuls 2 inches apart onto ungreased cookie sheets.

3. Bake 11 to 12 minutes or just until set. Cool on cookie sheets 1 minute. Remove to wire racks; cool completely. Store in tightly covered container up to 1 week.

Makes about 3½ dozen cookies

whole wheat chocolate sheet cake

2½ cups whole wheat flour
  1 cup sugar
  2 teaspoons cinnamon
  1 cup water
  ½ cup vegetable oil
  ¼ cup cocoa
1½ teaspoons baking soda
  1 cup buttermilk
  2 large eggs, beaten
  1 teaspoon vanilla

Icing
  ½ cup butter or margarine
  3 to 4 tablespoons low-fat milk
  3 cups confectioners' sugar
  1 teaspoon vanilla extract
  1 cup flaked coconut

Preheat oven to 350°F.

Cake

Mix flour, sugar and cinnamon together in a large bowl. Bring water, oil and cocoa to a boil. Pour over flour mixture and mix 1 minute, scraping bowl.

Dissolve soda in buttermilk, adding to mixture in bowl along with eggs and vanilla. Mix an additional 2 minutes.

Pour into greased and floured 15×10-inch pan. Bake 20 minutes. Ice cake if desired, while cake is still slightly warm.

Icing

In a saucepan, melt butter or margarine; add milk and heat. Boiling is not necessary. Remove from heat and add confectioners' sugar and vanilla extract; stir vigorously until smooth and glossy. Add more milk only if frosting isn't fluid enough to spread easily. Spread over slightly warm sheet cake and immediately sprinkle with coconut. When cake is cool, cut into 24 servings.   *Makes 24 servings*

Favorite recipe from **Wheat Foods Council**

whole wheat chocolate sheet cake

peanut butter jumbos

1½ cups peanut butter
   1 cup granulated sugar
   1 cup packed brown sugar
   ½ cup (1 stick) butter, softened
   3 eggs
   1 teaspoon vanilla
4½ cups uncooked old-fashioned oats
   2 teaspoons baking soda
   1 cup (6 ounces) semisweet chocolate chips
   1 cup candy-coated chocolate pieces

1. Preheat oven to 350°F. Lightly grease cookie sheets or line with parchment paper.

2. Beat peanut butter, granulated sugar, brown sugar, butter, eggs and vanilla in large bowl until well blended. Stir in oats and baking soda until well blended. Stir in chocolate chips and candy pieces. Drop dough by ⅓ cupfuls 4 inches apart onto prepared cookie sheets. Press each cookie to flatten slightly.

3. Bake 15 to 20 minutes or until firm in center. Remove to wire racks to cool.

Makes about 1½ dozen cookies

Peanut Butter Jumbo Sandwiches: Prepare cookies as directed. Place ⅓ cup softened chocolate or vanilla ice cream on cookie bottom. Top with another cookie. Lightly press sandwich together. Repeat with remaining cookies. Wrap sandwiches in plastic wrap; freeze until firm.

chocolate fruit and nut cookies

½ cup all-purpose flour
½ cup whole wheat flour
¼ cup unsweetened cocoa powder
½ teaspoon salt
½ teaspoon baking soda
½ cup (1 stick) butter, softened
½ cup granulated sugar
¼ cup packed light brown sugar
¼ cup vegetable oil
 1 egg, lightly beaten
 1 teaspoon vanilla
½ cup old-fashioned oats
¾ cup mixed dried fruit bits
¾ cup semisweet chocolate chunks
½ cup chopped mixed nuts

1. Preheat oven to 350°F. Lightly grease cookie sheets. Combine flours, cocoa, salt and baking soda in medium bowl.

2. Beat butter and sugars in large bowl with electric mixer until light and fluffy. Add oil, egg and vanilla; beat until well blended. Add flour mixture and oats; beat just until blended. Stir in fruit bits, chocolate chunks and nuts. Shape dough by heaping tablespoons into balls; place 2 inches apart on prepared cookie sheets.

3. Bake 12 to 14 minutes or until set and no longer shiny. Cool 2 minutes on cookie sheets. Remove to wire racks; cool completely.   *Makes about 3 dozen cookies*

chocolate fruit and nut cookies

oatmeal date bars

2 packages (18 ounces each) refrigerated oatmeal raisin cookie dough
2½ cups old-fashioned oats, divided
2 packages (8 ounces each) chopped dates
1 cup water
½ cup sugar
1 teaspoon vanilla

1. Preheat oven to 350°F. Lightly grease 13×9-inch baking pan. Let dough stand at room temperature about 15 minutes.

2. For topping, combine three fourths of one package of dough and 1 cup oats in medium bowl; beat until well blended. Set aside.

3. For crust, combine remaining 1¼ packages of dough and remaining 1½ cups oats in large bowl; beat until well blended. Press dough evenly onto bottom of prepared pan. Bake 10 minutes.

4. Meanwhile for filling, combine dates, water and sugar in medium saucepan; bring to a boil over high heat. Boil 3 minutes; remove from heat and stir in vanilla. Spread date mixture evenly over partially baked crust; sprinkle evenly with topping mixture.

5. Bake 25 to 28 minutes or until bubbly. Cool completely in pan on wire rack.

Makes about 2 dozen bars

Most oats are steamed and flattened to produce old-fashioned oats. The more they are flattened, the quicker they cook. The good news is that oats, unlike many other grains, retain their bran and germ after processing. So you'll get most of the same whole grain nutrition with quick oats or even instant oatmeal. That includes beta-glucan, a fiber found in oats that has been shown to help lower cholesterol.

earth day cookies

¾ cup packed dark brown sugar
½ cup (1 stick) butter, softened
¼ cup milk
1 egg
1 teaspoon vanilla
1 cup all-purpose flour
½ cup whole wheat flour
1 teaspoon baking powder
1 teaspoon cinnamon
½ teaspoon salt
¼ teaspoon baking soda
1 cup trail mix, coarsely chopped
½ cup old-fashioned oats

1. Preheat oven to 375°F.

2. Beat brown sugar and butter in large bowl with electric mixer until fluffy. Add milk, egg and vanilla; beat until combined.

3. Combine flours, baking powder, cinnamon, salt and baking soda in medium bowl. Gradually beat flour mixture into butter mixture. Stir in trail mix and oats. Drop tablespoonfuls of dough 2 inches apart onto cookie sheet.

4. Bake 10 to 12 minutes or until edges are lightly browned. *Do not overbake.* Remove to wire rack to cool. Store in airtight container.

Makes about 2½ dozen cookies

whole wheat oatmeal cookies

1 cup whole wheat flour
1 teaspoon ground cinnamon
1 teaspoon baking powder
½ teaspoon baking soda
½ teaspoon salt
1 cup packed light brown sugar
¼ cup unsweetened applesauce
2 egg whites
2 tablespoons butter, softened
1½ teaspoons vanilla
1⅓ cups quick oats
½ cup raisins

1. Preheat oven to 375°F. Lightly spray cookie sheets with nonstick cooking spray. Combine flour, cinnamon, baking powder, baking soda and salt in medium bowl; mix well.

2. Combine brown sugar, applesauce, egg whites, butter and vanilla in large bowl. Mix until small crumbs form. Add flour mixture; mix well. Fold in oats and raisins. Drop by rounded teaspoonfuls 2 inches apart onto prepared cookie sheets.

3. Bake 10 to 12 minutes or until golden brown. Cool on wire racks.

Makes 40 cookies

acknowledgments

The publisher would like to thank the companies and organizations listed below for the use of their recipes and photographs in this publication.

California Tree Fruit Agreement

Dole Food Company, Inc.

Grandma's®, A Division of B&G Foods, Inc.

JOLLY TIME® Pop Corn

Minnesota Cultivated Wild Rice Council

Mott's® is a registered trademark of Mott's, LLP

National Honey Board

National Onion Association

National Sunflower Association

Northwest Cherry Growers

The Quaker® Oatmeal Kitchens

RED STAR® Yeast, a product of Lasaffre Yeast Corporation

Riviana Foods Inc.

The Sugar Association, Inc.

USA Rice Federation™

Washington Apple Commission

Wheat Foods Council

Wisconsin Milk Marketing Board

VOLUME MEASUREMENTS (dry)

$1/8$ teaspoon = 0.5 mL
$1/4$ teaspoon = 1 mL
$1/2$ teaspoon = 2 mL
$3/4$ teaspoon = 4 mL
1 teaspoon = 5 mL
1 tablespoon = 15 mL
2 tablespoons = 30 mL
$1/4$ cup = 60 mL
$1/3$ cup = 75 mL
$1/2$ cup = 125 mL
$2/3$ cup = 150 mL
$3/4$ cup = 175 mL
1 cup = 250 mL
2 cups = 1 pint = 500 mL
3 cups = 750 mL
4 cups = 1 quart = 1 L

VOLUME MEASUREMENTS (fluid)

1 fluid ounce (2 tablespoons) = 30 mL
4 fluid ounces ($1/2$ cup) = 125 mL
8 fluid ounces (1 cup) = 250 mL
12 fluid ounces ($1 1/2$ cups) = 375 mL
16 fluid ounces (2 cups) = 500 mL

WEIGHTS (mass)

$1/2$ ounce = 15 g
1 ounce = 30 g
3 ounces = 90 g
4 ounces = 120 g
8 ounces = 225 g
10 ounces = 285 g
12 ounces = 360 g
16 ounces = 1 pound = 450 g

DIMENSIONS

$1/16$ inch = 2 mm
$1/8$ inch = 3 mm
$1/4$ inch = 6 mm
$1/2$ inch = 1.5 cm
$3/4$ inch = 2 cm
1 inch = 2.5 cm

OVEN TEMPERATURES

250°F = 120°C
275°F = 140°C
300°F = 150°C
325°F = 160°C
350°F = 180°C
375°F = 190°C
400°F = 200°C
425°F = 220°C
450°F = 230°C

BAKING PAN SIZES

Utensil	Size in Inches/Quarts	Metric Volume	Size in Centimeters
Baking or	$8 \times 8 \times 2$	2 L	$20 \times 20 \times 5$
Cake Pan	$9 \times 9 \times 2$	2.5 L	$23 \times 23 \times 5$
(square or	$12 \times 8 \times 2$	3 L	$30 \times 20 \times 5$
rectangular)	$13 \times 9 \times 2$	3.5 L	$33 \times 23 \times 5$
Loaf Pan	$8 \times 4 \times 3$	1.5 L	$20 \times 10 \times 7$
	$9 \times 5 \times 3$	2 L	$23 \times 13 \times 7$
Round Layer	$8 \times 1 1/2$	1.2 L	20×4
Cake Pan	$9 \times 1 1/2$	1.5 L	23×4
Pie Plate	$8 \times 1 1/4$	750 mL	20×3
	$9 \times 1 1/4$	1 L	23×3
Baking Dish	1 quart	1 L	—
or Casserole	$1 1/2$ quart	1.5 L	—
	2 quart	2 L	—